ONE BLOOD

THE BIBLICAL ANSWER TO RACISM

ONE BLOOD

THE BIBLICAL ANSWER TO RACISM

KEN HAM

CARL WIELAND

DON BATTEN

Master Books

First printing: November 1999
Ninth printing: April 2005

ISBN: 0-89051-276-0
Library of Congress Catalog Card Number: 99-67331

Note: All Scripture quoted is from the Modern King James Version unless otherwise noted.

Cover by Brandon Vallorani and Janell Robertson

Research/production team: Dave Jolly, Mark Looy, and Dan Zordel

Illustrations by Dan Lietha

Printed in the United States of America

Please visit our website for other great titles:
www.masterbooks.net

For information regarding publicity for author interviews contact the publicity department at (870) 438-5288.

CONTENTS

FOREWORD

One Blood promises to be revolutionary in its impact on the thinking of millions of people. When we look at the ugliness of racism and the impact of evolution, we realize there is a solution to the problem of racism — and that's biblical principles and scientific facts.

The prime reason I was thrilled to be asked to write this foreword is to share from my perspective why *One Blood* can be a life-changing experience for many people. First, as a practical matter, in the business world turnover of capable people is cost prohibitive. We have to rehire, retrain, and fit new employees into our work structure. That's time-consuming, frustrating, and expensive. When prejudice rears its ugly head and we miss out on capable people because they are not of our "race," it is particularly frustrating and often leads to expensive litigation. This happens because we treat people like we see them, and try as we might, our prejudice is perceived by the person who is treated in a less-than-equal manner. Needless to say, that person's loyalty will be shallow and short-lived.

Three Native Americans had huge impacts on my life: One on my sales career, another on my speaking career, and yet another on my spiritual walk. The

African American lady who spent the weekend of July 4, 1972, in our home is the reason I am a Christian today. My closest friend for the last 35 years is Jewish, and he was my first encourager when I launched my speaking career. My daughter-in-law is from Campeche, Mexico, and one of the key members of our staff is a native of India. Just think what I would have missed had I been racist!

As you read *One Blood*, I hope you will carefully check the Scriptures that are revealed and the scientific evidence that is presented. I believe it will remove virtually all of your prejudice. Of course, the real difficulty is a heart problem and not an intellect problem. As you read this book, follow through on the biblical admonitions and ask God to come into your heart in the person of Jesus Christ, because when our heart is right, then all of us is right.

Prejudice is frequently a matter of "what's best for me." Example: If you are prejudiced and white, but you need a heart transplant and the only one available is from a black man, would your prejudice still prevail, or would you be grateful for your life made possible by your black brother? Question: If you're a black man and your daughter is drowning and you are unable to save her, but a white man is available, would you turn him down and let your daughter drown? I don't think so.

This is reality. If your life, or the life of a loved one, were at stake, you would not care if your benefactor were black, white, brown, or yellow. You wouldn't even ask if he were Irish, Polish, Jewish, Gypsy, Italian, Eskimo, etc. Your gratitude for life would be the only thing on your mind. I hope you will remember that when you deal with those who are "different." In God's eyes, all of us are equally loved and equally important. Christ shed His blood to cover the sins of all of us.

Racism is morally, socially, scientifically, and biblically wrong. It is an ugly blot on our society, and *One Blood* clearly explains why we really are all one blood.

God bless you as you ponder this all-important question. I strongly encourage you to get extra copies of this book and give them to friends, family, and associates, because the less prejudice we have in this world of ours, the more peace, freedom, and opportunity all of us will have.

Zig Ziglar, Author/Motivational Teacher

PREFACE

The railroad car, once you realize what it represents, forces you in, although not in the same way the people it memorializes were forced aboard so many decades ago. The odd smell — which many visitors say must be the smell of death — can't be scrubbed away. It shouldn't be, for it reminds our senses in a visceral way of what happens when men leave God, and malevolent ideas go unchallenged.

This exhibit at the U.S. Holocaust Museum in Washington D.C. is part of the story of a man who hated other groups of people. The malevolent idea he used was evolution.

When Adolf Hitler looked for a "final solution" for what he called the "Jewish problem" — the fact of the Jews' existence — he had only to recall what scientists like Ernst Haeckel promoted and liberal theologians embraced: that a purposeless process, known as evolution, had generated all of life's complexity, including civilization itself. It had done so through a pitiless procedure of the strong eliminating the weak. As the influence of this idea spread, the Bible was increasingly taught as myth.

The Nazi leader convinced millions of his followers that this ethnic group was corrupt, weak, and therefore, deserving of extinction. The Holocaust, or *Shoah* in Hebrew, resulted, with millions of Jews packed into trains and transported to extermination camps.

He didn't stop, there, however. To Hitler, people with different skin color and facial features were "sub-human." These ideas came directly from the research of fanatical Darwinists like Haeckel, who had popularized the idea decades earlier that human fetuses go through their "evolutionary history" in the womb — from cell to fish to frog to monkey to man.

It also followed naturally from Darwin's idea that different people groups had been separated for many tens of thousands of years, slowly evolving what must therefore be major biological differences. Since evolution has no fixed pace, it is therefore natural to assume that one group is less highly evolved than another — i.e., less human. For the dictator of Nazi Germany, these anti-God ideas were a means to an end.

But if Haeckel, Darwin, Hitler, and all the rest are long dead, what does it mean for us today? Who cares? It happened so long ago, right?

But then we remember that our publishing headquarters are located a mere 30 miles from the international headquarters of the Ku Klux Klan, right in the middle of the United States. We also note that the so-called "Christian" Identity movement believes Jews are the offspring of Eve and Satan, and that blacks are not really human. Neo-Nazis are becoming a force in Germany. And, of course, there is "ethnic cleansing" (a euphemism for mass murder) going on all over the world as never before. In Australia, Aborigines — people who are as human and capable of achievement as any other — were thought until relatively recently to be sub-human. Thousands were deliberately murdered to provide specimens of "living missing links" for Northern Hemisphere museums. The Australian National Museum classified Aboriginal people under the heading "Australian animals" and gave instructions on how to plug up the bullet holes once you had shot your specimen for "science."

We hear rabid sports fans viciously question the intelligence level of black players who drop passes in the end zone or miss balls on a sun-drenched diamond. The evening news bulletins assault us with senseless killings, rapes, and other persecutions. And this racial hatred is not confined to white men hating brown, red, or yellow-skinned people. One only has to think of that notorious promoter of hate, Black Muslim leader Louis Farrakhan. Or anti-Chinese violence in Indonesia. Even the Japanese in World War II, to justify their nation's expansionist aggression, had been told that they were the most "highly evolved" race on earth. After all, Europeans, with their longer arms and hairier chests, were clearly still closer to the ape, weren't they?

There is no way to understand the cultural cancer of racism until we first seriously read the Bible. For this breathtaking collection of 66 books is completely silent on our own modern concept of "races." Tragically, blacks, orientals, whites — all of us — have been pushed into "boxes" (the metaphor for which is the stinking, grisly railroad car) and we have forgotten that God has "made of one blood all nations of men" (Acts 17:26).

The world has forgotten that truth! This revelation is so startling to many people encountered at Answers in Genesis seminars, it's clear we have come adrift from our moorings. God has told us very clearly that we are all very closely related, and He has made it possible for us to understand the scientific facts found in this book.

The battle of ethnic hate and violence is one of the biggest questions of our time. Billions of dollars are spent fighting it. Presidents consult civic and religious leaders. Oprah devotes entire programs to it. And to put it delicately, many fine Christian organizations lament racism and talk in terms of the races getting along, but they fail to present a biblical answer to a searching world.

Ask yourself honestly: Are we winning? Have we acknowledged the answer? The next time you think we are making progress with race relations in the usual way, remember when you heard someone call an intelligent athlete a "nigger." Remember the contempt otherwise reasonable white men have for "Japs." Remember that we have bashed the poor Neanderthals and questioned their intelligence (they had bigger brains than we do!) *because they looked different*. Remember the beastly dragging death of the man from Texas by white supremacists.

Then remember what's in your own heart.

There are "races" in the Bible, but they are spiritual journeys for us all to run (e.g., 1 Cor. 9:24). Only when we see God for who He is — and see who He meant for us to be — will we see our relatives (all other people) for what they are.

Then we will be able to climb out of the ghastly boxes into which we've forced ourselves.

We urge you to help *One Blood* travel far and wide, to let its crucial insights start a reformation in "race" relations.

Jim Fletcher
Editor-in-chief, Master Books

INTRODUCTION

I f all human beings who are alive or who have ever lived on earth are descendants of only two people, Adam and Eve, as a literal reading of Genesis would demand, then how do we account for all the different "races" of people? Shouldn't there be just one "race" of humans? How can all human beings be the descendants of just two people anyway? Also, where did Cain get his wife? Why do the "races" differ in such things as skin color and eye shape? Does the Bible allow "interracial" marriage?

These are just some of the many difficult questions people ask concerning the human race. There are, however, easy-to-understand answers that support the Bible's account of history. Let's start at the beginning, Genesis.

In Genesis 2 we read the detailed account of the creation of the first two people, Adam and Eve.[1] In Genesis chapter 4 we are told that Adam and Eve had three sons, Cain, Abel, and Seth. Thus, if Adam and Eve were the parents of the entire human race, where did, for example, Cain find a wife so there would be subsequent generations of people? It is perhaps the most-asked question we receive at Answers in Genesis, and it is the subject of chapter 1.

ENDNOTES

1   Michael J. Kruger. "An Understanding of Genesis 2:5," *Technical Journal*, vol. 11, no. 1, 1997, p. 106–110.

CAIN'S WIFE

Many skeptics have claimed that for Cain to find a wife, there must have been other "races" of people on the earth who were not descendants of Adam and Eve. To many people, this question is a stumbling block to accepting the creation account of Genesis and its record of only one man and woman at the beginning of history. This issue is also critical to the integrity of the gospel message, as we shall see. Read Genesis 4:1–5:5 for the necessary background to this topic:

> And Adam knew Eve his wife. And she conceived and bore Cain, and said, I have gotten a man from the Lord. And she bore again, his brother Abel. And Abel was a keeper of sheep, but Cain was a tiller of the ground.
> And in the end of days, it happened, Cain brought to the Lord an offering of the fruit of the ground. And Abel also brought of the

firstlings of his flock and of the fat of it. And the Lord had respect to Abel and to his offering, but He did not have respect to Cain and to his offering. And Cain glowed with anger, and his face fell. And the Lord said to Cain, Why have you angrily glowed? And why did your face fall? If you do well, shall you not be accepted? And if you do not do well, sin crouches at the door; and its desire is for you, and you shall rule over it.

And Cain talked with his brother Abel. And it happened when they were in the field, Cain rose up against his brother Abel and killed him. And the Lord said unto Cain, Where is your brother Abel? And he said, I do not know. Am I my brother's keeper? And He said, What have you done? The voice of your brother's blood cries to Me from the ground. And now you are cursed more than the ground which opened its mouth to receive your brother's blood from your hand. When you till the ground, it will not again give its strength to you. And you shall be a vagabond and a fugitive in the earth.

And Cain said to the Lord, My punishment is greater than I can bear. Behold! You have driven me out from the face of the earth today, and I shall be hidden from Your face. And I shall be a fugitive and a vagabond in the earth, and it shall be that anyone who finds me shall kill me.

And the Lord said to him, Therefore whoever kills Cain shall be avenged seven times. And the Lord set a mark upon Cain so that anyone who found him should not kill him.

And Cain went out from the presence of the Lord and lived in the land of Nod, on the east of Eden. And Cain knew his wife, and she conceived and bore Enoch. And he built a city, and called the name of the city after the name of his son, Enoch. And Irad was born to Enoch. And Irad fathered Mehujael. And Mehujael fathered Methusael. And Methusael fathered Lamech. And Lamech took two wives to himself. The name of the first one was Adah, and the name of the other was Zillah. And Adah bore Jabal; he was the father of those who dwell in tents, and with cattle. And his brother's name was Jubal; he was the father of all those playing the harp and the organ. And Zillah also bore Tubal-Cain, the hammerer of every engraving tool of bronze and iron. And the sister of Tubal-Cain was Naamah.

And Lamech said to his wives, Adah and Zillah, Hear my voice, wives of Lamech, listen to my speech. For I have killed a man because of my wound, and a young man because of my hurt. For Cain is avenged seven times, and Lamech seventy-seven times.

And Adam knew his wife again. And she bore a son, and called his name Seth. For she said, God has appointed me another seed instead of Abel, because Cain killed him. And there was also a son born to Seth, and he called his name Enos. Then men began to call upon the name of the Lord. This is the book of the generations of Adam. In the day that God

created man, he made him in the likeness
of God. He created them male and female,
and blessed them. And He called their name
Adam in the day when they were created.

And Adam lived one hundred and thirty
years and fathered a son in his own likeness,
after his own image. And he called his name
Seth. And the days of Adam after he had
fathered Seth were eight hundred years. And
he fathered sons and daughters. And all the
days that Adam lived were nine hundred and
thirty years. And he died (Gen. 4:1–5:5).

In order to answer the question "Where did Cain
get his wife?" we first need to cover some crucial
background information concerning the meaning of
the gospel. Consider Romans 5:12:

Wherefore, as by *one man* sin entered
into the world, and death by sin; and so death
passed upon all men, for that all have sinned.

We also read in 1 Corinthians 15:45 that Adam
was "the *first man.*" God did not start by making a
"batch" of men and women.

The Bible makes it clear that *only* the descendants of Adam can be saved. Romans 5 teaches that
we sin because Adam brought sin into the world.
The death penalty, which Adam received as judgment for his sin of rebellion, has also been passed
on to all his descendants.[1]

Since Adam was the head of the human race, when
he "fell," we who were "in the loins" of Adam "fell"
also. Thus, we are all separated from God. The final

consequence of sin would be separation from God in our sinful state forever. The good news, however, is that there is a way for us to return to God!

Because a man brought sin and death into the world, the human race (all descendants of Adam) needed a sinless Man to pay the penalty for sin and the resulting judgment of death. But the Bible teaches that "*all have sinned*" (Rom. 3:23, 5:12). What was the solution?

God provided the solution — a way to deliver man from his wretched state. Paul explains in 1 Corinthians 15 that God provided another Adam! The Son of God became a man — a *perfect* Man — yet still our relation! He is called "*the last Adam*" (1 Cor. 15:45), because He took the place of the first Adam. He became the "new head" and, because He was sinless, was able to pay the penalty for sin:

> For since death is through man, the resurrection of the dead also is through a Man. For as in Adam all die, even so in Christ all will be made alive (1 Cor. 15:21–22).

Christ suffered death (the penalty for sin) on the cross, shedding His blood ("and without shedding of blood is no remission," Heb. 9:22) so that those who put their trust in His work on the cross can come in repentance of their sin of rebellion (in Adam) and be reconciled to God.

Thus, only descendants of the first man Adam can be saved.

The Bible describes *all* human beings as sinners and as being *all* related: "And He has made all nations of men of one blood to dwell on all the face of the

Jesus Christ "The Last Adam"
1 Cor. 15:45

For as in Adam all die, even so in Christ shall all be made alive
1 Cor. 15:22

"The First Adam"
1 Cor. 15:45

earth" (Acts 17:26). The gospel only makes sense if all humans who have ever lived (except for the first woman) are descendants of the first man, Adam. Eve, in a sense, was a "descendant" of Adam in that she was made from his flesh and thus had some biological connection to him (Gen. 2:21–23). If this were not so, then the gospel could not be explained or defended.

Thus, there was only *one* man at the beginning — made from the dust of the earth (Gen. 2:7).

This also means that Cain's wife was a descendant of Adam. She couldn't have come from another "race" of people and must be accounted for from Adam's descendants.

In Genesis 3:20 we read, "And Adam called his wife's name Eve, because she was the mother of all living." In other words, all people other than Adam are descendants of Eve — she was the first woman.

Eve was made from Adam's side (Gen. 2:21–24) — this was a unique event. In the New Testament, Jesus (Matt. 19:4–6) and Paul (Eph. 5:31) use this historical and one-time event as the foundation for the marriage of one man and one woman.

Also, in Genesis 2:20 we are told that when Adam looked at the animals, he couldn't find a mate — there was no one of his kind.

All this makes it obvious *that there was only* one *woman, Adam's wife, from the beginning.* There could not have been other women who were not her descendants.

Thus, if Christians cannot defend that all humans (including Cain's wife) can trace their ancestry ultimately to Adam and Eve, then how can they understand and explain the gospel? How can they justify sending missionaries to every tribe and nation? One needs to be able to answer the question of Cain's wife to illustrate that Christians can defend the gospel and all that it teaches.

Cain was the first child of Adam and Eve recorded in Scripture (Gen. 4:1). He and his brothers, Abel (Gen.

4:2) and Seth (Gen. 4:25), were part of the *first* generation of children ever born on this earth. Even
though these three males are specifically mentioned,
Adam and Eve had other children.

In Genesis 5:4 we read a statement that sums
up the life of Adam and Eve: "And the days of Adam
after he had fathered Seth were eight hundred years.
And he fathered sons and daughters."

During their lives, Adam and Eve had a number of male and female children. In fact, the Jewish
historian Josephus wrote, "The number of Adam's
children, as says the old tradition, was thirty-three
sons and twenty-three daughters."[2]

Scripture doesn't tell us how many children were
born to Adam and Eve, but considering their long
life spans — Adam lived for 930 years (Gen. 5:5) —
it would seem logical to suggest there were many!
Remember, they were commanded to "Be fruitful,
and multiply" (Gen. 1:28).

If we now work totally from Scripture, without
any personal prejudices or other extra-biblical ideas,
then back at the beginning, when there was only the
first generation, brothers would have had to marry sisters or there wouldn't have been any more generations!

We're not told when Cain married or many of
the details of other marriages and children, but we
can say for certain that Cain's wife was either one of
his sisters or another close relative.

Many people immediately reject the conclusion
that Adam and Eve's sons and daughters married each
other by appealing to the law against brother-sister
intermarriage. Some say that you can't marry your
relation. Actually, if you don't marry your relation,
you don't marry a human! A wife is related to her

ONE BLOOD

Acts 17:26

Adam & Eve
1 Corinthians 15:45
Genesis 3:20

Sons & Daughters
Genesis 5:4

Noah & Sons
Genesis 9:17-19

People at Tower of Babel
Genesis 11:8-9

Different People Groups/Cultures

husband before they are married because *all* people are descendants of Adam and Eve — all are of *one blood.* Remember that Abraham was married to his half-sister (Gen. 20:12). God's law prohibited such marriages (Lev. 18–20), but that law was given to Moses some 400 years later. Provided marriage was one man with one woman for life, there was no

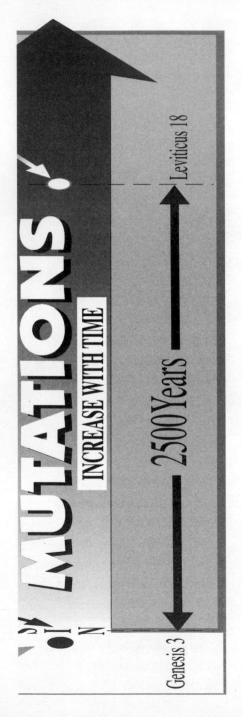

MUTATIONS!

INCREASE WITH TIME

2500 Years

Leviticus 18

Genesis 3

disobedience to God's law originally (before the time of Moses) when close relatives (even brothers and sisters) married each other.

Today, brothers and sisters (and half-brothers and half-sisters, etc.) are not permitted by law to marry and have children. Now it is observed that children produced in a union between brother and sister have a greater chance of being deformed or mentally retarded. As a matter of fact, the closer the couple are in relationship, the *more* likely it is that any offspring will be deformed. Most people know this, but many are unaware of the easily understood mechanism involved.

Each person inherits a set of genes

from his or her mother and father. Unfortunately, genes today contain many mistakes (because of sin and the Curse), and these mistakes show up in a variety of ways. For instance, research has linked many serious diseases to these mistakes — cystic fibrosis and hemophilia, for example. Less serious physical deformities may also be caused by these mistakes — for example, a missing nasal septum, shortsightedness, and so on. Let's face it: the main reason we call

For we know that the whole creation groaneth

and travaileth in pain together until now.

Romans 8:22

each other normal is because we agree to do so!

Children inherit two sets of genes — one set from each parent. A brother and sister are likely to have similar mistakes in their genes because they are inherited from the same parents. If there were a union between such a brother and sister that produced offspring, the mistakes could pair together, resulting in two bad copies of a gene and such things as mental retardation and/or deformities in the children.

Conversely, the further away the parents are in relationship to each other, the more likely it is that they will have *different* mistakes in their genes. Children, inheriting one set of genes from each parent, are likely to end up with some of the pairs of genes containing one bad gene in each pair. The good gene tends to override the bad so that a deformity (a serious one, anyway) does not occur. Often the person carries the bad gene without any obvious defect. (Overall, though, the human race is slowly degenerating as mistakes — errors in copying DNA, called mutations — accumulate, generation after generation.)

This fact of present-day life, however, did not apply to Adam and Eve. When the first two people were created, they were perfect. Everything God made was "very good" (Gen. 1:31). That means their genes were perfect — no mistakes! But, when sin entered the world because of Adam (Gen. 3:6), God cursed the world so that the perfect creation then began to degenerate — that is, suffer death and decay (Rom. 8:22). Over a long period of time, this degeneration would have resulted in all sorts of mistakes occurring in the genetic material of living things.

Cain was in the first generation of children ever born. He (as well as his brothers and sisters) would have received virtually no imperfect genes from Adam or Eve, since the effects of sin and the Curse would have been minimal to start with. In that situation, brother and sister could have married (provided it was one man for one woman — which is what marriage is all about — Matt. 19:4–6) without any potential to produce deformed offspring.

By the time of Moses (about 2,500 years later), degenerative mistakes would have accumulated to such an extent in the human race that it would have been necessary for God to bring in the laws forbidding brother-sister (and close relative) marriage (Lev. 18–20).[3] Also, there were plenty of people on the earth by now, so close relations did not have to marry.

In all, there appear to be three inter-related reasons for the introduction of laws forbidding close intermarriage:

> 1. As we have already discussed, there was the need to protect against the increasing potential to produce deformed offspring.
> 2. God's laws were instrumental in keeping the Jewish nation strong, healthy, and within the purposes of God.
> 3. These laws were a means of protecting the individual, the family structure, and society at large. The psychological damage caused by parent/child incestuous relationships should not be minimized.

CAIN AND THE LAND OF NOD

Some claim that the passage in Genesis 4:16–17 means that Cain went to the land of Nod and found a

wife. Thus, they conclude there must have been another race of people on the earth, who were not descendants of Adam, who produced Cain's wife.

> And Cain went out from the presence of
> the Lord and lived in the land of Nod, on the
> east of Eden. And Cain knew his wife, and
> she conceived and bore Enoch. And he built
> a city, and called the name of the city after
> the name of his son, Enoch (Gen. 4: 16–17).

From what has been stated above, it is clear that
all humans, Cain's wife included, are descendants of
Adam. However, this passage does *not* say that Cain
went to the land of Nod and found a wife. John Calvin
in commenting on these verses states: "From the context we may gather that Cain, before he slew his
brother, had married a wife; otherwise Moses would
now have related something respecting his marriage."[4]
Cain was married *before* he went to the land
of Nod. He didn't find a wife there, but "knew"
(i.e., had sexual relations with) his wife there.[5]

> Behold! You have driven me out from
> the face of the earth today, and I shall be
> hidden from Your face. And I shall be a fu-
> gitive and a vagabond in the earth, and it
> shall be that anyone who finds me shall kill
> me (Gen. 4:14).

Some claim that there had to be lots of people
on the earth other than Adam and Eve's descendants,
otherwise Cain wouldn't have been fearful of people
wanting to slay him because he killed Abel.

First of all, why would a stranger want to kill Cain? Only a close relative of Abel would care enough.

Secondly, Cain and Abel were born quite some time before the event of Abel's death. Genesis 4:3 states: "And in process of time it came to pass, that Cain brought of the fruit of the ground an offering unto the Lord."

Note the phrase "*in the process of time.*" We know Seth was born when Adam was 130 years old (Gen. 5:3), and Eve saw him as a "replacement" for Abel (Gen. 4:25). Therefore, the time period from Cain's birth to Abel's death may have been 100 years or more — allowing plenty of time for other children of Adam and Eve to marry and have children. By the time Abel was killed, there may have been a considerable number of descendants of Adam and Eve, making up several generations.

Some claim that for Cain to go to the land of Nod and build a city, he would have required a lot of technology that must have already been in that land, presumably developed by other "races." Adam and Eve's descendants, however, were very intelligent people. We are told that Jubal made musical instruments such as the harp and organ (Gen. 4:21), and Tubal-Cain worked with brass and iron (Gen. 4:22).

Because of intense evolutionary indoctrination, many people today have the idea that their generation is the most "advanced" that has ever lived on this planet. Just because we have jet airplanes and computers doesn't mean we are the most advanced in intelligence. Modern technology is really a result of the accumulation of knowledge.

We must remember that our brains have suffered from 6,000 years (since Adam) of the Curse. We have

Our Thinking In Every Area

Illustration by Rick Wood

greatly degenerated compared to people many generations ago. We may be nowhere near as intelligent or inventive as Adam and Eve's children. Scripture gives us a glimpse of what appears to be relatively advanced technology almost from the beginning. Cain had the knowledge and talent to know how to build a city!

There is another angle to this: the Hebrew word translated "city" does not necessarily suggest a huge metropolis. Rather, it could merely mean a place guarded by a watch.[6] This would make sense for a person fearful of someone taking his life.

Genesis is the record of the God who was there as history happened. It is the Word of One who knows everything, and who is a reliable witness from the past. Thus, when we use Genesis as a basis for understanding history, we can make sense of evidence that would otherwise be a real mystery. You see, if evolution is true, science has an even bigger problem than Cain's wife to explain — namely, how could man ever evolve by mutations (mistakes) in the first place, since that process would have made everyone's children deformed?[7] The mere fact that people can produce offspring that are *not* largely deformed is a testimony to creation, not evolution.

Now that we've solved the perceived "problem"

of Cain's wife, and how subsequent generations of people could descend from the first two people, how can we explain the seemingly major differences among people groups around the world? How can we account for all the different "races" if we are all descended from Adam and Eve? What has caused changes like the different skin colors for example?

Before we can answer these questions, we need to understand some basic principles of genetics. To do this, we will consider the changes that we observe in animals (particularly among dogs). We will then apply our understanding of the science of genetics to the human kind. At the same time, we will learn that true science in the present does not support the evolutionary view of origins, but confirms the biblical account.

ENDNOTES

1   If one reads the Bible from Genesis to Revelation, interpreting Scripture with Scripture, then the conclusion is that death, bloodshed, disease, and suffering of the "nephesh" animals and man only came into existence after Adam sinned. When Christians accept the supposed millions of years for the age of the fossils, then they undermine the gospel by accepting death, violence, disease, bloodshed, and suffering before sin. The Bible makes it clear that everything was "very good" at the end of the sixth day of creation. The world could not have been full of diseases like cancer at that time — and yet such diseases are evident in the fossil bones supposedly millions of years old. More information on this topic can be found in the following articles:

Ken Ham, "The Necessity for Believing in Six Literal Days," *Creation*, vol. 18, no. 1, December 1995–February 1996, p. 38–41.

Ken Ham, "Millions of Years and the 'Doctrine of Balaam,' " *Creation*, vol. 19, no. 3, June–August 1997, p. 15–17.

Ken Ham, "A Young Earth — It's *Not* the Issue!" *Answers in Genesis Newsletter*, vol. 5, no. 1, January 1998, p. 1–4.

Darren H. Tanke and Bruce M. Rothschild, "Paleopathology," *Encyclopedia of Dinosaurs* (San Diego, CA: Academic Press, 1997), p. 525–530.

B.M. Rothschild, D. Tanke, and Ken Carpenter, "Tyrannosaurs Suffered from Gout," *Nature*, vol. 387, no. 6631, May 22, 1997, p. 357.

2 Flavius Josephus (translated by William Whiston, A.M.), *The Complete Works of Josephus* (Grand Rapids, MI: Kregel Publications, 1981, p. 27.

3 Some have claimed this means God changed His mind by changing the laws. But God didn't change His mind — God never changes. Because of the changes that sin brought, He introduced new laws for our sake.

4 John Calvin, *Commentaries on the First Book of Moses Called Genesis* (Grand Rapids, MI: Baker Book House, 1979), Vol. 1, p. 214.

5 Even if Calvin's suggestion concerning this matter is not correct, there was still plenty of time for numerous descendants of Adam and Eve to move out and settle areas such as the land of Nod.

6 *Strong's Concordance* (Peabody, MA: Hendrickson Publishers, 1990), 5892, (Hebrew and Chaldee Dictionary p. 88): "a *city* (a place guarded by *waking* or a watch) in the widest sense (even of a mere *encampment* or *post*)."

7 Natural selection does *not* automatically get rid of harmful mutations, since most are only exposed to selection when they are "homozygous" — i.e., inherited from both parents. So the progressive accumulation of mutational "load" is a very real problem for evolutionary theories.

CHAPTER 2

NATURAL SELECTION AND SPECIATION

I n Genesis chapter 1, we read that God created the animals and plants *after their kind.* The phrase "after its kind" or "after their kind" occurs a total of ten times in Genesis 1. Thus, God's Word is explaining to us that God created distinct *kinds* of animals and plants — each to reproduce after its own kind.

Now, evolutionists teach that one kind of animal changed into another over millions of years. They claim that the observable changes in living animals and plants are evidence that evolution is occurring today.

The truth is, however, that these observable changes fit exactly with what the Bible teaches concerning "kinds" and are the *opposite* of the changes required by evolution.

STRAW MAN

People often get confused about this issue because evolutionists set up a straw man scenario. For instance, at the entrance to the Darwinian exhibit at the Natural History Museum in London, one is confronted with the following statements: "Before Charles Darwin, most people believed that God created all living things in exactly the form that we see them today. This is the basis of the doctrine of Creation. . . . Darwin's work supported the view that all living things have developed into the forms we see today by a process of gradual change over long periods of time. This is what is meant by evolution."[1]

Now, creationists do not believe that God made the animals and plants just as we see them today. For instance, when God made dogs, He didn't make a poodle! After all, dogs like poodles are in fact degenerate mutants, suffering the effects of 6,000 years of the Curse.

Creationists agree that animals and plants change. For instance, dogs change, but they change into different varieties or breeds of dogs. We observe many different dogs such as dingoes, wolves, coyotes, and the numerous domestic varieties like poodles, St. Bernards, and so on. How then did these varieties of wild and domestic dogs come about? And how does a creationist explain these changes that have occurred in dogs?

GENETICS

To understand this, let's consider the dog/wolf "kind" in more detail. To begin with, we need to consider some very basic principles from the science of genetics.[2] Even though in reality it's much more complicated than this, the principles are still the same and

DOGS DO CHANGE...

INTO DIFFERENT DOGS!
"After their kind" Genesis 1

thus provide us with a basic understanding.

The master program that determines that a dog is a dog, as well as a poodle variety of dog, is carried in its genes. A dog/wolf has tens of thousands of genes.[3] We need to understand that creatures inherit two copies of each gene — one from each parent. The two copies can be different — then they are called different "alleles." An offspring can get only one of each gene pair from each parent. Let us consider gene-pairs represented as "A" "a" "B" "b" "C" and "c." Now, let's imagine God makes the original dog/wolf kind, a male and a female, each having three pairs of genes in the following combination:

Aa Bb Cc

From these two dogs we can get many different combinations in the offspring. For example, the mating of:

Aa Bb Cc (male dog) x Aa Bb Cc (female dog)

can produce 27 different combinations of these genes in the offspring. Consider the following five:

VARIATION WITHIN THE DOG KIND

Dog Parents

MALE
Aa Bb Cc

x

FEMALE
Aa Bb Cc

Possible information in egg/sperm cells:

A a B b C c

Offspring

Possible combinations in offspring:

AA BB CC
aa bb cc
AA Bb CC
Aa BB Cc
Aa Bb Cc

Note that each of the five offspring all have dog genes obtained from their parents. However, they each have a different combination of genes than the parents. Thus, even though they are still dogs, they will each look slightly different from each other and from the parents.

Now, just to help you understand how much variability God built into the genes, consider the human kind. Scientists have estimated that if it were physically possible, just two human parents could produce far more children than atoms in the known universe without getting two the same — such is the variation possible just from different combinations of the existing genes. That is an incredible amount of in-built variability.[4]

FORMATION OF NEW "SPECIES"

Now let's consider a scenario in history. Two members of the dog/wolf kind that God had selected to be on Noah's ark got off this enormous ship in the Middle East after the Flood. These dogs mated and had offspring, and then these mated and had more offspring, and so on. Eventually, small groups of dogs started splitting away from the main group and went off by themselves in different directions. As a result, small populations of dogs were separated from each other. This obviously split up the gene pool, resulting in a number of populations with different combinations of genes.

Some of the combinations resulted in features that are better able to survive in a particular environment. For instance, in a cold climate, dogs which carried more of the genes for thick furry coats would survive better than their companions that had less of a coat, but still

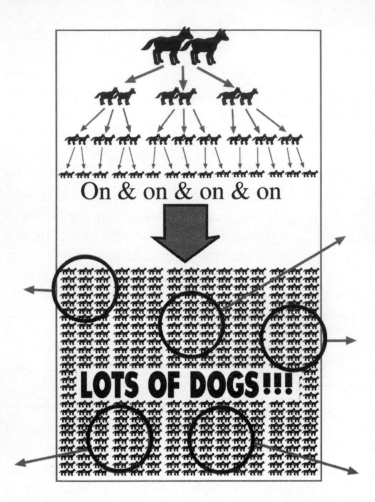

On & on & on & on

LOTS OF DOGS!!!

had some for thin fur. So the thick-furred dogs were more likely to survive and pass on those genes. In time, the population might end up only having genes for thick fur and none for thin. So these dogs have become specialized (adapted) to cold areas. But this situation does not explain "molecules-to-man" evolution because this population has come about through natural selection getting *rid* of the genes that code for thin fur.

By this process of splitting the original gene pool further and further, with natural selection "favoring" certain types for different environments, distinct varieties — even new "species" — could arise, all inheriting their features from that original dog kind on the ark, but in different combinations and subsets. Thus, over time, dingoes, wolves, coyotes, etc., arose. This is a great example of natural selection in action, but it is *not* evolution in the sense that people understand that word — there is no process operating which *adds information* to the populations, which is what is needed to turn a reptile into a bird, for example.

Actually such speciation, as we call it, can happen quite rapidly. Biologists today know of a principle called the "founder effect," where small subsets of a population get isolated and so the descendants of these subsets have a different genetic composition from the main population, with less information. They are also aware that such things as genetic drift and "jumping genes" can result in quite rapid speciation. But again, in no case is new genetic information created, just transferred from one place on the genome to another, for example.

Mutations are the other supposed mechanism

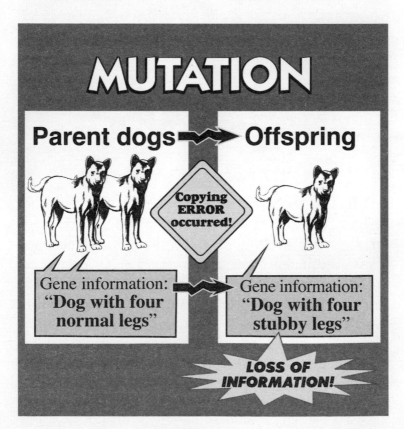

for evolution. When the genes are copied by the parent to pass on to the offspring, sometimes an error is made. This error in copying is one kind of mutation. Like typing errors, mutations "mess up" the information, that is, they cause a loss of information. So it is not surprising that mutations in humans are known to cause thousands of diseases. They certainly do not add new functional genes, but they can contribute to variations arising through decreasing the effectiveness of existing genes. Such changes can also contribute to speciation — for example, a disparity in size or behavior can result in breeding isolation.

A definition of a species is that it does not breed with other species — that is, it is isolated in a breeding sense. Note the following:

> 1. Natural selection can only operate on the information in the gene pool — the original created information in the particular kind, plus some defective genes, caused by mutations.
>
> 2. Over a period of time there is loss of information. For instance, the aa bb cc combination has *lost* the As, Bs, and Cs. Domestic breeds tend to have many of their gene pairs the same; for example, aabbcc. This means that the offspring are almost identical to their parents, with little variation possible — they are therefore called "pure breeds." All domestic varieties have less genetic information (and thus variability) than the original "wild" types from which they were bred. In addition, many of the features in domestic dogs are the result of harmful mutations,

which would not survive well in the wild, but are "selected for" by humans.

3. There is no mechanism by which new information is added into the genes.[5] Dr. Werner Gitt, a professor from Germany and an expert in information theory, stated that "there is no known law of nature, no known process and no known sequence of events which can cause information to originate by itself in matter."[6]

Mutations do not increase the amount of information, as is required by evolution. As biophysicist Dr. Lee Spetner (who was a fellow at Johns Hopkins University) stated, "All point mutations that have been studied on the molecular level turn out to reduce the genetic information and not to increase it." He went on to say, "Not even one mutation has been observed that adds a little information to the genome."[7]

Although there are rare "beneficial" mutations, these always involve downhill changes. Note that sometimes a defect can be a benefit. For example, if beetles on a windy island inherit a mutation that makes them wingless, they are less likely to be blown into the sea and drowned.

Mutations occur because of the Curse that resulted from the judgment because of sin, recorded in Genesis 3. Because the Curse has operated in this world for around 6,000 years, there are now lots of mutations affecting the genes of living things.

THE DOG KIND

WOLF

COYOTE

DINGO

COLLIE

POODLE

LESS INFORMATION

NO NEW INFORMATION ADDED!

4. Over time, specialization can occur, as varieties become very separated. They can even get to the stage that, even though they are from the same kind, they can no longer interbreed. Genetically, they are much worse off because now they can't mix with others of their own kind to regain the original variability they once had.

EVOLUTION DOESN'T WORK

For an evolutionary mechanism to change a reptile into a bird, for instance, there would have to be processes observed in true science to add new information into the genes (for example, information on how to make feathers). However, the changes observed with both natural selection and mutations are the opposite of those needed for evolution to work.

Scientists know this is true but, sadly, it is not public knowledge nor is it usually explained to students in schools or colleges. For instance, in 1980 at the Field Museum of Natural History in Chicago, many of the world's leading evolutionary experts gathered for a conference on evolution. A leading science writer summarized one of the conclusions of these discussions:

> The central question of the Chicago conference was whether the mechanisms underlying micro-evolution [the term used to describe the observable small changes in animals and plants] can be extrapolated to explain the phenomena of macro-evolution [the term used to describe the major changes necessary to change a reptile into a bird or ape-like creature into man]. At the risk of doing violence to the positions of some of the people at the meeting, the answer can be given as a clear, *No*. [emphasis added].[8]

Darwin was correct about natural selection — we do observe small changes in living things, and many new species of animals and plants have arisen. However, now that we understand more about the science of genetics, we know that the processes of natural selection and mutation can never form new *kinds* of animals or plants, but only new *species* or *varieties* within the *same* kind.

It's interesting to note that "progressive creationists" (who accept the belief of billions of years of earth's history) accuse biblical young-earth creationists of believing in evolution, because of their understanding of speciation as described above. For instance, Hugh Ross states:

> Ironically, creation scientists (quietly) propose an efficiency of natural biological evolution greater than even the most optimistic Darwinist would dare to suggest. . . . While creation scientists call themselves anti-evolutionists, they do not reject natural biological evolution as impossible in principle.[9]

The more speciation is studied, however, the more scientists realize that many factors are involved, and that there are acknowledged mechanisms that can result in this process occurring quite rapidly.[10] And these mechanisms, as has been shown, in essence are the opposite of those required for molecules-to-man evolution.

To fit with their acceptance of billions of years of earth's history, progressive creationists believe that God created millions of species over millions of years. Thus, they do not want to accept the understood mechanisms of speciation that can explain the rapid development of species and varieties of land animals since the flood of Noah's day, less than 5,000 years ago.

At the same time, progressive creationists

recognize that the genealogies demand a very recent history for the human race. Thus, they need to be able to explain the diversity of characteristics within the different people groups within a short period of time. Because of a rejection of observed biological mechanisms, they have no answer except to say God must have created them this way.

For instance, Hugh Ross concedes, "The origin of humanity's different racial groups remains a mystery." He then goes on to say, "Neither the Bible nor extrabiblical literature nor modern scientific research offers a direct explanation. . . . How did the human species develop such direct skin colors and other more subtle differences in the relatively brief time from the days of Noah to the days of Moses? The usual answer that it happened in response to natural selection seems inadequate. Genetic and anthropological research shows that natural selection cannot work as rapidly as necessary to offer a plausible explanation."

Thus, even though Hugh Ross admits he could be accused of a "God-of-the gaps" approach, he states that after the Tower of Babel, "God may have done more than diversify language at that time. He possibly may have introduced some external change — those we recognize as racial distinctives."[11]

Progressive creationists get into such dilemmas because of their compromise of adding billions of years to the Bible.

We will now show how accepting the science of genetics and the current understanding of the mechanisms of speciation very simply explains the origin of the "races" within the biblical time frame.

ENDNOTES

1 London Natural History Museum, Darwin exhibit as viewed in 1997.

2 Founded by the creationist scientist Gregor Mendel.

3 Genes are very complex, each comprising thousands of "letters" of genetic code.

4 Francisco Ayala, "The Mechanisms of Evolution," *Scientific American,* vol. 239, no. 3, September 1978, p. 48–61.

5 Ayala. "The Mechanisms of Evolution," p. 65.
   N. Seppa, "Ulcer Bacterium's Drug Resistance Unmasked," *Science News*, April 25, 1998, p. 262.
   Ed Struzik and Dr. Kinga Kowalewska-Grochowska, "Ancient Bacteria Revived," *Sunday Herald*, September 16, 1990.

6 Werner Gitt, *In the Beginning Was Information* (Bielefeld, Germany: CLV, 1997), p. 64–67, 79, 107.

7 Lee Spetner, *Not by Chance* (New York: Judaica Press, 1998), p. 138, 159–160.

8 Roger Lewin, "Evolutionary Theory Under Fire," *Science*, vol. 210, November 21, 1980, p. 883.

9 Hugh Ross, *The Genesis Question* (Colorado Springs, CO; NavPress, 1998), p. 151.

10 Carl Wieland, "Brisk Biters," *Creation*, vol. 21, no. 2, March–May 1999, p. 41.

11 Ross, *The Genesis Question*, p. 177.

CHAPTER 3

GENETICS AND THE HUMAN FAMILY

Let us now apply this basic understanding of genetics to human beings. How did all the different "races" arise (from Noah's family)? First, what constitutes a "race?"

In the 1800s, before Darwinian evolution was popularized, most people, when talking about "races," were referring to such groups as the "English race," "Irish race," and so on. However, this all changed when Charles Darwin published his book *On the Origin of Species by Means of Natural Selection or the Preservation of Favoured Races in the Struggle for Life*.

Darwinian evolution was (and still is) inherently a racist philosophy, teaching that different groups or "races" of people evolved at different times and rates, so some groups are more like their ape-like ancestors than others. The Australian Aborigines, for instance, were considered to be the missing links between an ape-like ancestor and the rest of mankind.[1] This resulted in terrible prejudices and injustices towards the Australian Aborigines.[2] A leading evolutionary spokesperson, Stephen Jay Gould, stated that "Biological arguments for racism may have been common before 1850, but they increased by orders of magnitude following the acceptance of evolutionary theory."[3]

Racist attitudes fueled by evolutionary thinking were largely responsible for an African pygmy actually being displayed, along with an orangutan, in a cage in the Bronx Zoo.[4]

As a result of Darwinian evolution, many people started thinking in terms of the different people groups around the world representing different "races," but within the context of evolutionary philosophy. This has resulted in many people today, consciously or unconsciously, having ingrained prejudices against certain other groups of people.

All human beings in the world today, however, are classified as *Homo sapiens sapiens*. Scientists today admit that, biologically, there really is only one race of humans. For instance, a scientist at the Advancement of Science Convention in Atlanta in 1997 stated, "Race is a social construct derived mainly from perceptions conditioned by events of recorded history, and it has no basic biological reality." This person went on to say, "Curiously enough, the idea comes very close to being of American manufacture."[5]

Reporting on research conducted on the concept of race, the American ABC News science page stated, "More and more scientists find that the differences that set us apart are cultural, not racial. Some even say that the word 'race' should be abandoned because it's meaningless." The article went on to say that "we accept the idea of race because it's a convenient way of putting people into broad categories, frequently to suppress them. . . . The most hideous example was provided by Hitler's Germany. And racial prejudice remains common throughout the world."[6]

In a 1998 article in the *Journal of Counseling and Development*, researchers argued that the term "race" is basically so meaningless that it should be discarded.[7]

Because of the influences of Darwinian evolution and the resulting prejudices, we believe everyone (and especially Christians) should abandon the term "races." We could refer instead to the different "people groups" around the world.

THE BIBLE AND "RACE"

The Bible does not even use the word "race" in reference to people,[8] but does describe all human beings as being of "one blood" (Acts 17:26). This, of course, emphasizes that we are all related, for all humans are descendants of the first man Adam (1 Cor. 15:45).[9] Because Jesus Christ also became a descendant of Adam, being called the "last Adam" (1 Cor. 15:45), the gospel should be preached to all tribes and nations. When Jesus Christ became a man (God-man), He became a descendant of Adam. Thus, He became our relative — totally man, a descendant of the first Adam, yet totally God. Any descendant of Adam can be saved, because our mutual relative by blood (Jesus Christ) died and rose again.

"RACIAL" DIFFERENCES

Some people think there must be different "races" of people because there appear to be major differences between various groups, such as skin color and eye shape.

The truth, though, is that these so-called "racial characteristics" are only minor variations among the people groups. Scientists have found that if one were to take any two people from anywhere in the world, the basic genetic differences between these two people would typically be around 0.2 percent — even if they came from the same people group.[10] But, these so-called "racial" characteristics that many think are major differences (skin color, eye shape, etc.) account for only 6 percent of this 0.2 percent variation, which amounts to a mere 0.012 percent difference genetically.[11]

In other words, the so-called "racial" differences are absolutely trivial. Overall, there is more variation *within* any group than there is *between* one group and another. If a white person is looking for a tissue match for an organ transplant, for instance, the best match may come from a black person, and vice versa. The

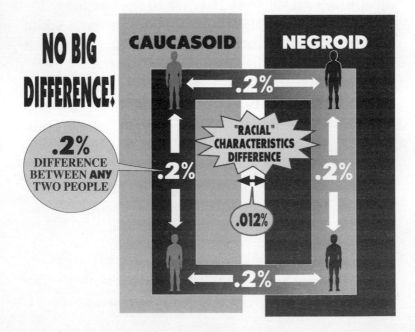

ABC News science page stated, "What the facts show is that there are differences among us, but they stem from culture, not race."[12]

The only reason many people think these differences are major is because they've been brought up in a culture that has taught them to see the differences this way.

According to the Bible, all people on earth today descended from Noah and his wife, his three sons and their wives, and before that from Adam and Eve (Gen. 1–11). The Bible tells us how the population that descended from Noah's family had one language and were living together and disobeying God's command to *"fill the earth"* (Gen. 9:1; 11:4).[13] God confused their language, causing a break-up of the population into smaller groups which scattered over the earth (Gen. 11:8–9).

Using modern genetics, we will show how, following such a break-up of a population, variations in skin color, for example, can develop in only a few generations. And there is good evidence to show that the various groups of people we have today have *not* been separated for huge periods of time.[14]

ENDNOTES

1   A.S. Brown, "Missing Links with Mankind in Early Dawn of History," *New York Tribune*, February 10, 1924, p. 11.

2   Carl Wieland, "Darwin's Body Snatchers," *Creation*, vol. 14, no. 2, March–May 1992, p. 16–18 (see chapter 10, also).

3   Stephen Jay Gould, *Ontogeny and Phylogeny* (Cambridge, MA: Belknap-Harvard Press, 1977), p. 127–128.

4   Jerry Bergman, "Ota Benga: The Man Who Was Put on Display in the Zoo!" *Creation*, vol. 16, no. 1, December 1993–February 1994, p. 48–50. (See chapter 10 for the shocking details.)

5   Robert Lee Hotz, "Race Has No Basis in Biology, Researchers Say," *Los Angeles Times* article reprinted in the *Cincinnati Enquirer*, February 20, 1997, p. A3.

6   "We're All the Same," American Broadcasting Corporation News, September 10, 1998, www.abcnews.com/sections/science/DyeHard/dye72.html.

7   Susan Chavez Cameron and Susan Macias Wycoff, "The Destructive Nature of the Term Race: Growing Beyond a False Paradigm," *Journal of Counseling & Development*, vol. 76, 1998, p. 277–285.

8   The NIV does use the word in two places. However, in Ezra 9:2 the Hebrew is literally "seed," and in Romans 9:3 the phrase "those of my own race" is, in the original Greek, literally "my relatives according to the flesh" (KJV: "my kinsmen according to the flesh").

9   Ken Ham, *Where Did Cain Get His Wife?* (Florence, KY: Answers in Genesis, 1997).

10 J.C. Gutin, "End of the Rainbow," *Discover*, November 1994, p. 72–73.

11 Cameron and Wycoff, "The Destructive Nature of the Term Race: Growing Beyond a False Paradigm, p. 277-285.

12 "We're All the Same," ABC News, September 10, 1998.

13 The KJV says "replenish the earth," but replenish simply meant "fill" when the KJV was translated. The word has changed its meaning. See Charles Taylor, "What Does 'Replenish the Earth' Mean?" *Creation*, vol. 18, no. 2, March–May 1996, p. 44–45.

14 Worldwide variations in mitochondrial DNA (the "Mitochondrial Eve" story) were claimed to show that all people today trace back to a single mother (living in a small population) 70,000 to 800,000 years ago. Recent findings on the rate of mitochondrial DNA mutations shortens this period drastically to put it within the biblical time frame. See L. Lowe and S. Scherer, "Mitochondrial Eve: The Plot Thickens," *Trends in Ecology and Evolution,* vol. 12, no. 11, 1997, p. 422–423; C. Wieland, "A Shrinking Date for Eve," *CEN Technical Journal,* vol. 12, no. 1, p. 1–3.

CHAPTER 4

ONE RACE

There is really only one race — the human race. Scripture distinguishes people by tribal or na-tional groupings, not by skin color or physical appearances. Clearly, though, there are groups of people who have certain features (e.g., skin "color") in common, which distinguish them from other groups. As stated earlier, we prefer to call these "people groups" rather than "races."

All peoples can freely interbreed and produce fertile offspring. This shows that the biological differences between the "races" are not very great at all. In fact, the DNA differences are trivial, as already pointed out.

Anthropologists generally classify people into a fairly small number of main racial groups, such as the Caucasoid (European or "white"[1]), the Mongoloid (which includes the Chinese and the American Indians), the Negroid (black Africans), and the Australoid (the Australian Aborigines). Within each classification, there may be many different sub-groups.

Virtually all evolutionists would now agree that the various people groups did not have separate origins; that is, in the evolutionary belief system, the different people groups did not each evolve from a different group of animals. So they would agree with biblical creationists that all people groups have come from the same original population. Of course, they believe that such groups as the Aborigines and the Chinese have had many tens of thousands of years of separation. Most people believe that there are such vast differences between groups that there *had* to be many years for these differences to somehow develop.

One reason for this is that many people believe that the observable differences come from some people having unique features in their hereditary make-up which others lack. This is an understandable but incorrect idea. Let's look at skin color, for instance. It is easy to think that since different groups of people have yellow skin, red skin, black skin, white skin, and brown skin, there must be many different skin pigments or colorings. And since different chemicals for coloring would mean a different genetic recipe or code in the hereditary blueprint in each people group, it appears to be a real problem. How could all those differences develop within a short time?

Here's how. We all have the same coloring pigment in our skin: melanin. This is a dark brownish pigment that is found in special cells in our skin. If we have *none* (as do people called albinos, who suffer from an inherited mutation-caused defect, so they lack the ability to produce melanin), then we will have a very white or pink skin coloring. If we produce a little melanin, it means that we will be European white. If our skin produces a great deal of melanin, we will be a very deep black. And in between, of course, are all shades of brown. There are no other significant skin pigments.[2]

In summary, from currently available information, the really important factor in determining skin color is melanin — the amount produced.

This situation is true not only for skin color. Generally, whatever feature we may look at, no people group has anything that is, in its essence, uniquely different from that possessed by another. For example, the Asian, or almond-shaped, eye gets its appearance

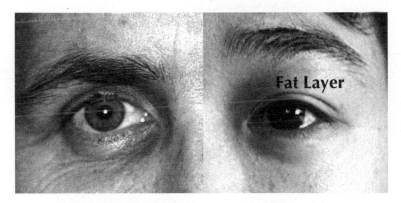

Caucasian eye   **Asian eye**

The Asian eye differs from the Caucasian and black African eye in having more orbital fat.

simply by having an extra fold of fat. Both Asian and Caucasian eyes have fat — the latter simply have less of it.

What does melanin do? It protects the skin against damage by ultraviolet light from the sun. If you have too little in a very sunny environment, you will more easily suffer from sunburn and skin cancer. If you have a great deal of melanin, and you live in a country where there is little sunshine, it is much harder for your body to get adequate amounts of vitamin D (which needs sunshine for its production in your body). You may then suffer from vitamin D deficiency, which could cause a bone disorder such as rickets.

We also need to be aware that one is not born with a genetically fixed amount of melanin, but rather with a genetically fixed *potential* to produce a certain amount, increasing in response to sunlight. For example, if you are in a Caucasian community, you may have noticed that when your friends headed for the beach at the very beginning of summer, they may, if they spent their time indoors during winter, have all been more or less the same pale white. As the summer went on, however, some became much darker than others.

But how do we explain the formation of many different shades of skin color arising in such a short biblical time scale (a few thousand years)? Let's look at a few observations that can help us to explain this. From here on, whenever we use such words as "different colors," we are, strictly speaking, referring to different shades of the one color, melanin.

If a person from a very black people group marries someone from a very white group, their offspring (called "mulattos") are mid-brown. It has long been known that when mulattos marry each other, their offspring may be virtually any "color," ranging from very black to very white. Understanding this gives us the clues we need for our overall question, so we must first look, in a simple way, at some of the basic facts of heredity.

HEREDITY

Each of us carries information in our body that describes us similar to the way a blueprint describes a finished building. It determines not only that we will be human beings, rather than cabbages or crocodiles, but also whether we will have blue eyes, short nose, long legs, etc. When a sperm fertilizes an egg, *all* the information that specifies how the person will be built (ignoring such superimposed factors as exercise and diet) is already present. This information is in coded form in our DNA.[3] To illustrate coding, a piece of rope with beads on it can carry a message in Morse code.

Can you see how the piece of rope, by using a simple sequence of short beads, long beads, and spaces

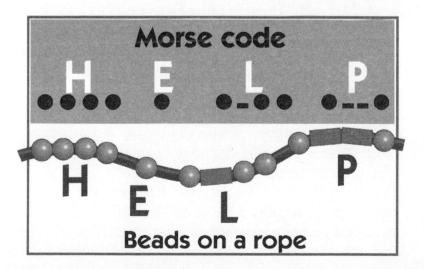

(to represent the dots and dashes of Morse code) can carry the same information as the English word "help" typed on a sheet of paper? The entire Bible could be written thus in Morse code on a long enough piece of rope.

In a similar way, the human blueprint is written in a code (or language convention), which is carried on very long chemical strings called DNA. This is by far the most efficient information storage system known, surpassing any foreseeable computer technology.[4] This information is copied (and reshuffled) from generation to generation as people reproduce.

The word "gene" refers to a small part of that information which carries the instructions for manufacturing only one enzyme, for example.[5] A small portion of the "message string," with only one specification on it, would be a simple way of understanding this gene concept.

For example, there is a gene that carries the instructions on how to make hemoglobin, the chemical (protein) which carries oxygen in your red blood cells. (Actually, there is more than one gene for hemoglobin, but that does not alter the principles of this necessarily simplified illustration.) If that gene has been damaged by mutation (such as when there are copying mistakes during reproduction), the instructions will be faulty, so it will make a crippled form of hemoglobin, if any. (There are a number of diseases, such as sickle-cell anemia and thalassaemia, which result from such mistakes.)

So, going back to that cell, and that egg which has just been fertilized — where does all of its information, its genes, come from? One-half has come from the father (carried by the sperm), and the other half

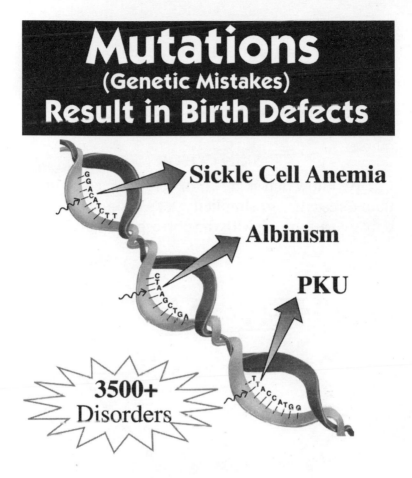

Mutations
(Genetic Mistakes)
Result in Birth Defects

Sickle Cell Anemia

Albinism

PKU

3500+ Disorders

from the mother (carried in the egg). Genes come in matching pairs, so in the case of hemoglobin, for example, we have *two* genes, which both contain the code (instruction) for hemoglobin manufacture, one from the mother and one from the father.

This is a very useful arrangement, because if you inherit a gene from one parent that is damaged and can instruct your cells to produce only a defective hemoglobin, you are likely to get a normal one from the other parent which will continue to give the right instructions. Thus, only half the hemoglobin in your body will be defective. (In fact, each of us carries hundreds of mistakes, inherited from one or the other of our parents, which are usually covered up by being matched with a normal gene from the other parent — this was discussed earlier.)

SKIN COLOR

We know that skin "color" is governed by more than one gene. For simplicity, let's assume there are only two,[6] A and B, with the correspondingly "more

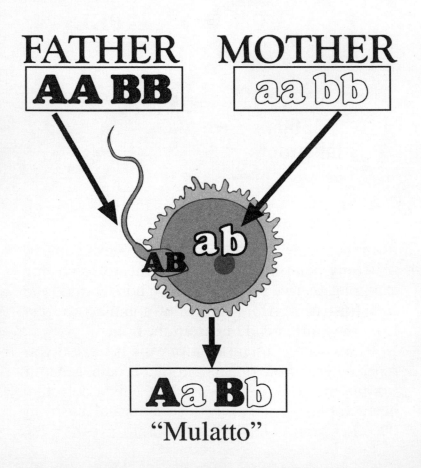

FATHER   **MOTHER**

AA BB   aa bb

AB ab

AaBb

"Mulatto"

silent" genes a and b. The small letters in this case will code for a small amount of melanin in the skin. So, a very dark group of people which, on intermarriage, kept producing only very dark offspring, would be AABB; the same situation for a very fair-skinned people would be aabb. The illustration on the preceding page shows what combinations would result in a mulatto (the offspring of an AABB and aabb union).

What would happen, using the Punnett square, if two such mid-brown mulatto people were to marry (the shading of the squares roughly indicates the resultant skin color)?

Surprisingly, we find that an entire range of "colors," from very white to very black, can result in only *one generation*, beginning with this particular type of mid-brown parents.

Those children born with AABB, who are pure black (in the sense of consistently having no other types of offspring), have no genes for lightness at all. If they were to marry and migrate to a place where their offspring could not intermarry with people of lighter color, all their children would be black — a pure "black line" would result.

Those with aabb are white. If they marry other whites and migrate to a place where their offspring cannot marry darker people, a pure (in the same sense) "white line" will result — they have lost genes that give them the ability to be black, that is, to produce a large amount of melanin.

So you can see how it is easily possible, beginning with two middle-brown parents, to get not only all the "colors," but also people groups with stable coloring. But what about people groups that are permanently middle-brown, such as we have today? Again, this is easily explained. Those of aaBB or AAbb, if they no longer interact with others, will be able to produce only mid-brown colored offspring. (You may want to work this out with your own Punnett square.)

If these lines were to interbreed again with other such lines, the process would be reversed. In a short time, their descendants would show a whole range of "colors," often in the same family. The photo on the following page shows what were called Britain's "most amazing twins." One is obviously light, the other obviously darker-skinned.

MIXED DOUBLES

Two-tone twins

Of course, this is not amazing at all when you do the exercise on paper, based on what we have discussed. (A clue if you want to do it yourself: mother cannot be AABB.) Also, the twins are obviously not identical twins (monozygous), which are derived from the same egg.

If all the humans on earth were to intermarry freely and then break into random groups that kept to themselves, a whole new set of combinations could emerge. It may be possible to have almond eyes with black skin, blue eyes with black, tightly curled hair, etc. We need to remember, of course, that the way in which genes express themselves is turning out to be much more complex than this simplified picture. Sometimes certain genes are linked together. However, the basic point is unaffected.

Even today, close observation shows that within a particular people group you will often see a feature normally associated with another group. For instance, you will occasionally see a European with a broad flat nose, or a Chinese person with very pale skin, or Caucasian eyes. As pointed out previously, most biologists now agree that among modern humans, "race" has little or no biological meaning. This also argues strongly against the idea that the people groups have been evolving separately for long periods.

WHAT REALLY HAPPENED?

We can now reconstruct the true history of the "people groups" using:

- The information given by the Creator himself in the Book of Genesis
- The background information given above
- Some consideration of the effect of the environment

The first man, Adam, from whom all other humans are descended, was created with the best possible combination of genes — for skin "color," for example. A long time after creation, a worldwide flood destroyed all humans except a man called Noah, his wife, his three sons, and their wives. This flood greatly changed the environment. Afterwards, God commanded the survivors to multiply and cover the earth (Gen. 9:1). A few hundred years later, men chose to disobey God and to remain united in building a great city, with the Tower of Babel as the focal point of rebellious worship.

From Genesis 11, we understand that up to this time there was only one language. God judged the people's disobedience by imposing different languages on man, so that they could not work together against God, and so that they were forced to scatter over the earth as God intended.

So all the "people groups" — "black" Africans, Indo-Europeans, Mongols, and others — have come into existence since that time. Some people sadly have promoted the false idea that dark skin is related to the so-called but non-existent curse of Ham. See chapter 6 for details on this topic.

Noah and his family were probably mid-brown, with genes for both dark and light skin, because a medium skin "color" would seem to be the most generally suitable (dark enough to protect against skin cancer, yet light enough to allow vitamin D production). As all the factors for skin "color" were present in Adam and Eve, they would most likely have been mid-brown as well. In fact, most of the world's population today is still mid-brown.

After the flood, for the few centuries until Babel, there was only one language and one culture group. Thus, there were no barriers to marriage within this group. This would tend to keep the skin "color" of the population away from the extremes. Very dark and very light skin would appear, of course, but people tending in either direction would be free to marry someone less dark or less light than themselves, ensuring that the average "color" stayed roughly the same.

The same would be true of other characteristics,

SHADES of SKIN COLOR

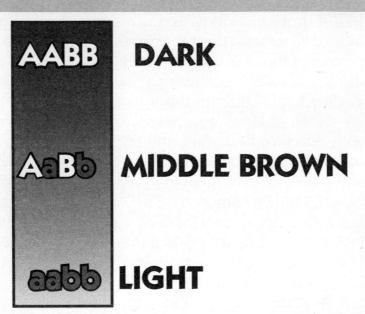

A	**LOTS OF MELANIN**
B	**LOTS OF MELANIN**
a	**SMALL AMOUNT OF MELANIN**
b	**SMALL AMOUNT OF MELANIN**

AABB **DARK**

AaBb **MIDDLE BROWN**

aabb **LIGHT**

not just skin "color." Under these sorts of circumstances, distinct, "constant" differences in appearance will never emerge. This is true for animals as well as human populations, as every biologist knows. To obtain such separate lines, you would need to break a large breeding group into smaller groups and keep them separate; that is, not interbreeding any more.

THE EFFECTS OF BABEL

This is exactly what happened at Babel. Once separate languages were imposed, there would have been instantaneous barriers. Not only would people tend not to marry someone they couldn't understand, but entire groups which spoke the same language would have difficulty relating to and trusting those which did not. They would tend to move away or be forced away from each other, into different environments. This latter, of course, is what God intended. But this intention could not have included keeping "different races" apart — there were no such recognizable groups yet!

It is unlikely that each small group would carry the same broad range of skin "colors" as the original, larger group. So one group might have more "dark" genes, on average, while another might have more "light" genes. The same thing would happen to other characteristics: nose shape, eye shape, etc. And since they would interbreed only within their own language group, this tendency would no longer be averaged out as before.

As these groups migrated away from Babel, they encountered new and different climate zones. This would also have affected the balance of inherited factors in the population, although the effects of the environment are not nearly as important as the genetic mix with which each group began. As an example, let us look at people who moved to cold areas with little sunlight. In those areas, the dark-skinned members of any group would not be able to produce enough vitamin D, and thus would be less healthy and have fewer children.

So, in time, the light-skinned members would

predominate. If several different groups went to such an area, and if one group happened to be carrying few genes for lightness, this particular group could in time die out. This natural selection acts on the characteristics *already present,* and does not evolve new ones.

It is interesting to note that in the Neanderthals of Europe (an extinct variety of man now recognized as fully human[7]), many showed evidence of vitamin D deficiency in their bones. In fact it was this, plus a large dose of evolutionary prejudice, which helped cause them to be classified as "ape-men" for a long time. It is thus quite plausible to suggest that they were a dark-skinned people group who were unfit for the environment into which they moved because of the skin-color genes *they began with.* Notice that this natural selection, as it is called, does not *produce* skin "colors," but only acts on the created "colors" that are *already there.*

Conversely, fair-skinned people in very sunny regions could easily be affected by skin cancer, in which case dark-skinned people would more readily survive.

So we see that the pressure of the environment can (a) affect the balance of genes within a group, and (b) even eliminate entire groups. This is why we see, to a large extent, a fit of characteristics to their environment (e.g., Nordic people with pale skin, equatorial people with dark skin, etc.).

But this is not always so. An Inuit (Eskimo) has brown skin, yet lives where there is not much sun. Presumably they have a genetic makeup such as AAbb which would not be able to produce lighter skin. On the other hand, native South Americans living on the equator do not have black skin. These examples show that natural selection does not create new information — if the genetic makeup of a group of people does not allow variation in "color" toward the desirable, natural selection cannot create such variation.

African Pygmies live in a hot area, but rarely experience strong sunshine in their dense jungle environment, yet they have dark skin.

Pygmies may be a good example of another factor that has affected the racial history of man: discrimination. If a variation from the normal occurs (e.g., a very light person among a dark people), then historically it has been usual for that person to be regarded as abnormal and unacceptable. Thus, such a person would find it hard to get a marriage partner. People could also recognize the poor fitness of certain characteristics in their environment, and so these become incorporated into the selection criteria for marriage partners. This would further tend to eliminate light genes from a dark people near the equator, and dark genes from light people at high latitudes. In this way, groups have tended to "purify" themselves.

Also, in some instances, inbreeding in a small group can highlight any commonly occurring unusual features that would previously have been swamped by continual intermarriage. There is a tribe in Africa whose members all have grossly deformed feet as a result of this inbreeding.

To return to Pygmies, if people possessing genes for short stature were discriminated against, and a small group of them sought refuge in the deepest forest, their marrying only each other would ensure a Pygmy "race" from then on. The fact that Pygmy tribes have never been observed to have their own languages, but instead speak dialects of neighboring non-Pygmy languages, is good evidence in support of this.

THE EFFECTS OF CHOICE

People groups that were already equipped with certain characteristics may have made deliberate (or semi-deliberate) choices concerning the environments to which they migrated. For instance, people with gene combinations for a thicker, more insulating layer of fat under their skin would tend to leave areas that were uncomfortably hot.

OTHER EVIDENCE

The evidence for the Bible's account of human origins is more than just biological and genetic. Since all peoples descended from Noah's family after the flood a relatively short time ago, we would be surprised if, in the stories and legends of many of the groups, there was not some memory, albeit distorted by time and retelling, of such a catastrophic event. In fact, an overwhelming number of cultures do have such an account of a world-destroying flood. Often these have startling parallels to the true, original account (eight people saved in a boat, a rainbow, the sending of the birds, and more).[8]

The following very brief excerpt is from just one of the many Australian Aboriginal dreamtime legends that are no doubt changed records of the flood account as given in Genesis:

> Long, long ago, before the great flood. . . . Then came the flood . . . tops of the mountains standing up above it like islands. The water kept on rising, and finally even the mountain peaks disappeared. The world was one vast, flat sheet of water, and there was no place for the Nurrumbunguttias to live. . . .

Slowly the flood waters receded. The mountaintops appeared again, and the spear heads of trees showed above the water. The sea went back into its own place, and the land steamed under the hot sun. . . . Animals, birds, insects, and reptiles appeared once more and made their homes on the quickly-drying plains.[9]

Some legends even mention three brothers (possibly the three sons of Noah?):

Unlike the majority of ancestors, who were products of the land they occupied, Yahberri, Mahmoon, and Birrum came from a distant land. The three brothers, together with their grandmother, arrived in a canoe made from the bark of the hoop pine tree, goondool.[10]

In summary, the dispersion at Babel, breaking a large interbreeding group into small, inbreeding groups, ensured that the resultant groups would have different mixes of genes for various physical features. By itself, this would ensure, in a short time, that there would be certain fixed differences in some of these groups, commonly called "races." In addition, the selection pressure of the environment would modify the existing combinations of genes, causing a tendency for characteristics to suit their environment.

There has been no simple-to-complex evolution of any genes, for the genes were present already. The dominant features of the various people groups result from different combinations of previously existing created genes, plus some minor changes in the direction of degeneration, resulting from mutation (accidental changes which can be inherited). The originally created (genetic) information has been either reshuffled or has degenerated, not been added to.

As one researcher put it, "It's kind of like if all of us are recipes. We have the same ingredients, maybe

SAME BASIC "RECIPE"
SLIGHT VARIATIONS

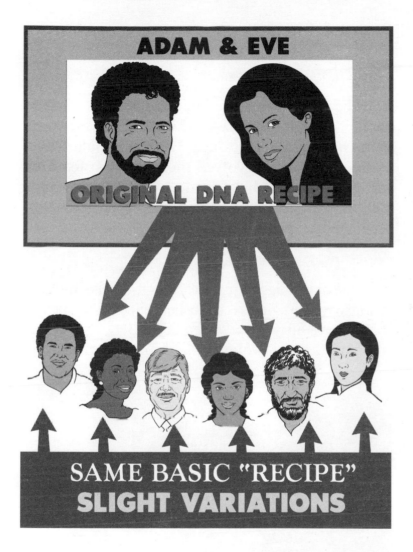

in different amounts, no matter what kind of cake we turn out to be."[11] In other words, just as someone can take a cake mix and make a number of different cakes, all with the same basic recipe, but slight variations — so we can think of Adam and Eve as having the original DNA recipe if you like, and all their descendants have the same basic "recipe" with slight variations.

CONSEQUENCES OF FALSE BELIEFS ABOUT THE ORIGIN OF "RACES"

• *Rejection of the gospel*

The accuracy of the historical details of Genesis is crucial to the trustworthiness of the Bible and to the whole gospel message.[12] So the popular belief that people groups evolved their different features, and could not all have come from Noah's family (contrary to the Bible), has eroded belief in the gospel of Jesus Christ.

• *Racism*

One of the biggest justifications for racial discrimination in modern times is the belief that, because people groups have allegedly evolved separately, they are at different stages of evolution, and some people groups

EVOLUTIONARY ANCESTOR

AUSTRALOID

NEGROID

MONGOLOID

CAUCASOID

RACES

The *wrong* view of human origins

are less evolved. Thus, the other person may not be as fully human as you. This sort of thinking inspired Hitler in his quest to eliminate Jews and Gypsies and to establish the "master race." Sadly, some Christians have been infected with racist thinking through the effects on our culture of evolutionary indoctrination, that people of a different "color" are inferior because they are supposedly closer to the animals.[13]

For instance, consider the way in which people in America were indoctrinated in ideas that fueled prejudice and racism towards certain groups of people.

In 1907, a *Scientific American* article stated:

> The personal appearance, characteristics, and traits of the Congo Pygmies . . . [conclude they are] small, apelike, elfish creatures. . . . They live in dense tangled forest in absolute savagery, and while they exhibit many ape-like features in their bodies. . . .[14]

Books such as *The History of Creation* by Ernst Haeckel were studied in the universities in the late 19th and early 20th centuries. Students read such things as:

> Nothing, however, is perhaps more remarkable in this respect, than that some of the wildest tribes in southern Asia and eastern Africa have no trace whatever of the first foundations of all human civilization, of family life, and marriage. They live together in herds, like apes, generally climbing on trees and eating fruits; they do not know of fire, and use stones and clubs as weapons, just like the higher apes. . . . At the lowest stage of

human mental development are the Australians, some tribes of the Polynesians, and the Bushmen, Hottentots, and some of the Negro tribes.[15]

And in 1924, the then *New York Tribune* newspaper carried an article about the Tasmanian Aboriginals, declaring: "Missing Links With Mankind in Early Dawn of History."[16]

Imagine what the people of England thought when they read an article in the *New Lloyd's Evening Post* about two Australian Aboriginals who were brought back to England:

> They appear to be a race totally incapable of civilization . . . these people are from a lower order of the human race.[17]

No wonder racist attitudes abound throughout countries like America and other nations.

• *Influence on Missionary Outreach*

Historically, the spread of evolutionary belief was associated with a slackening of fervor by Christians to reach the lost in faraway countries. The idea of savage, half-evolved inferior peoples somehow does not give rise to the same missionary urgency as the notion that our "cousins," closely linked to us in time and heredity, have yet to hear the gospel. Even many of the finest of today's missionary organizations have been influenced, often unconsciously, by this deeply ingrained belief in the evolutionary view of how other peoples and their religions came about.

ALL TRIBES AND NATIONS ARE DESCENDANTS OF NOAH'S FAMILY!

The Bible makes it clear that any newly "discovered" tribe is not a group of people who have never had any superior technology or knowledge of God in their culture. Rather, their culture began with (a) a knowledge of God, and (b) technology at least sufficient to build a boat of ocean-liner size. In looking for the reasons for some of this technological loss and cultural degeneration (see chapter 9), Romans 1 suggests that it is linked to the deliberate rejection by their ancestors of the worship of the living God.

A full appreciation of this would mean that, for such a group, we would not see the need to educate several generations and give them technical aid as a first priority, but would see their real and urgent need for the gospel as first and foremost.

In fact, most "primitive" tribes still have a memory, in their folklore and religion, of the fact that their ancestors turned away from the living God, the Creator. Don Richardson, missionary of *Peace Child* fame, has shown that a missionary approach, unblinded by evolutionary bias, and thus looking for this link and utilizing it, has borne a bountiful and blessed harvest on many occasions.[18]

For instance, consider the following excerpt from a book on Australian Aborigine dreamtime legends. Notice the similarity to the account of the forbidden fruit and the Fall in Genesis. It can bring tears to one's eyes to realize these people once had the truth of the Genesis account:

> The first man ever to live in Australia was Ber-rook-boorn. He had been made by Baiame.

After establishing Ber-rook-boorn and his
wife in a place that was good to live in, he
put his sacred mark on a yarran tree nearby,
which was the home of a swarm of bees.
"This is my tree," he told them, "and these
are my bees. You can take food anywhere you
like in the land I have given you, but this tree,
the bees, and the honey they make, you must
never touch. If you do, much evil will befall
you and all the people who will come after
you." . . . But one day, when the woman was
gathering firewood, her search carried her to
Baiame's tree. . . . A brooding presence
seemed to hover above her, and she raised her
eyes once more. Now that she was closer to
the tree she saw the bees hovering round the
trunk, and drops of honey glittering on the
bark. She stared at them, fascinated by the
sight. She had tasted the sweet excretion only
once before, but here was food for many
meals. She could not resist the lure of the shin-
ing drops. Letting her sticks fall to the ground,
she began to climb the tree. Suddenly there
was a rush of air and a dark shape with huge
black wings enveloped her. It was Narahdarn
the bat, whom Baiame had put there to guard
his yarran tree. Ber-rook-boorn's wife
scrambled down and rushed to her gunyah,
where she hid in the darkest corner. The evil
she had done could never be remedied. She
had released Narahdarn into the world, and
from that day onwards he became the symbol
of the death that afflicts all the descendants

of Ber-rook-boorn. It was the end of the golden age for Ber-rook-boorn and his wife.[19]

Jesus Christ, God's reconciliation in the face of man's rejection of the Creator, is the only truth that can set men and women of *every* culture, technology, people group or "color," truly free (John 8:32; 14:6).

Thus, the answer to racism is to believe and apply the history of the human race as given in Scripture. If every person were to accept that:

> They are all equal before God,
> All humans are descendants of Adam,
> All people are sinners in need of salvation,
> Everyone needs to receive Jesus Christ as Savior and Lord of their life,
> Each person must build his or her thinking on God's Word,
> All behaviors, attitudes, beliefs, etc. should be judged against the absolutes of God's Word, no matter what culture one is from —

then the problem of racism would be solved.

PEOPLE WITHOUT SOULS?

Sadly, though, once again the progressive creationists have to resort to anti-biblical explanations for the differences in the human race, because of their compromise with billions of years. For instance, once one accepts the notion of billions of years of earth's history, then that idea somehow has to be fitted into the Bible's time frame of history.

Progressive creationists recognize that they can't put millions of years into the genealogies from Adam to Christ, or they would make nonsense of them. The genealogies are there to show us that Christ can be traced back to the first Adam — after all, He is the "last Adam." Therefore, they have to place these millions of years before Adam.

Now the problem is this: These same dating methods they accept as absolute, "date" human skeletons back nearly two million years. Because of this compromise, they have to account for numerous human beings before Adam. Hugh Ross therefore proposes:

> Starting about two to four million years ago, God began creating man-like mammals or "hominids." These creatures stood on two feet, had large brains, and used tools. Some even buried their dead and painted on cave walls. However, they were very different from us. They had no spirit. They did not have a conscience like we do. They did not worship God or establish religious practices. In time, all these man-like creatures went extinct. Then, about 10 to 25 thousand years ago, God replaced them with Adam and Eve.[20]

If this is true, however, then think through the implications. According to the same types of dating methods the progressive creationists accept as absolute, the Australian Aborigines and American Indians are dated back 40,000 to 60,000 or more years ago. Thus, to be consistent, Ross would have to label these people as not being descendants of Adam and Eve (thus, they would have no souls).

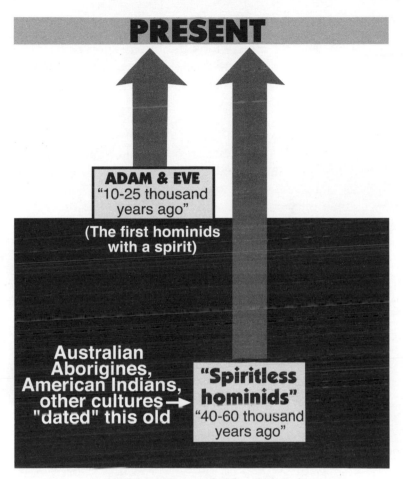

A wrong view of Aborigines!

Again, when someone adds man's opinions (e.g., millions of years) to the Bible, then one has to distort biblical truth and come up with fanciful stories to account for their compromise.

ENDNOTES

1 However, people inhabiting the Indian subcontinent are mainly Caucasian and their skin color ranges from light brown to quite dark. Even within Europe, skin color ranges from very pale to brown.

2 Other substances can in minor ways affect skin shading, such as the colored fibers of the protein elastin and the pigment carotene. However, once again we all share these same compounds, and the principles governing their inheritance are similar to those outlined here. Factors other than pigment in the skin may influence the shade perceived by the observer in subtle ways, such as the thickness of the overlying (clear) skin layers, the density and positioning of the blood capillary networks, etc. In fact, "melanin," which is produced by cells in the body called melanocytes, consists of two pigments, which also account for hair color. Eumelanin is very dark brown, phaeomelanin is more reddish. People tan when sunlight stimulates eumelanin production. Redheads, who are often unable to develop a protective tan, have a high proportion of phaeomelanin. They have probably inherited a defective gene which makes their pigment cells "unable to respond to normal signals that stimulate eumelanin production." See P. Cohen, "Redheads Come Out of the Shade," *New Scientist,* vol. 147, no. 1997, p.18.

3 Most of this DNA is in the nucleus of each cell, but some is contained in mitochondria, which are outside the nucleus in the cytoplasm. Sperm contribute only nuclear DNA when the egg is fertilized, so mitochondrial DNA is generally inherited only from the mother, via the egg.

4 Dr. Werner Gitt, "Dazzling Design in Miniature." *Creation,* vol. 20, no. 1, December 1998–February 1999, p. 6.

5 Incredibly, sometimes the same stretch of DNA can be "read" differently, to have more than one function. The creative intelligence behind such a thing is mind-boggling.

6 This simplification is not done to help our case — the more genes there are, the easier it is to have a huge range of "different" colors. The principle involved can be understood from using two as an example.

7   For a detailed examination and refutation of the so-called "ape-men," see Dr. Marvin Lubenow, *Bones of Contention* (Grand Rapids, MI: Baker Books, 1992).

8   A.W. Reed, *Aboriginal Fables and Legendary Tales* (Sydney, Australia: A.H. & A.W. Reed Pty. Ltd., 1965).
    A.W. Reed, *Aboriginal Legends: Animal Tales* (Frenchs Forest, NSW, Australia: A.H. & A.W. Reed Pty. Ltd., 1980).
    A.W. Reed, *Aboriginal Myths: Tales of the Dreamtime* (Chatswood, NSW, Australia: A.H. & A.W. Reed Pty. Ltd., 1980).
    A.W. Reed, *Aboriginal Stories of Australia* (A.H. & A.W. Reed Pty. Ltd., Frenchs Forest, NSW, Australia, 1980).
    A.W. Reed, *More Aboriginal Stories of Australia* (Sydney, Australia: A.H. & A.W. Reed Pty. Ltd., 1980).

9   Reed, *Aboriginal Fables and Legendary Tales*, p. 34–35.

10 Reed, *Aboriginal Myths: Tales of the Dreamtime*, p. 70.

11 "We're All the Same," www.abcnews.com, science page, 9/10/98.

12 Ken Ham, *The Lie: Evolution* (Green Forest, AR: Master Books, Inc., 1987).

13 Of course racism pre-dated Darwinian evolution: "The heart *is* deceitful above all *things*, and desperately wicked" (Jer. 17:9), but firstly, there were evolutionary theories around long before Darwin, and secondly, Darwinism gave a seeming scientific respectability to racism. The bottom line is that pre-Darwinian racism was equally contradicted by the biblical history of mankind.

14 Arthur H. J. Keane, "Anthropological Curiosities; the Pygmies of the World," *Scientific American*, Supplement 1650, vol. 64, no. 99, 1907, p. 107–108.

15 Ernst Haeckel, *The History of Creation: Or the Development of the Earth and its Inhabitants by the Action of Natural Causes,* translated by Prof. E. Ray Lankester (London: Henry S. King & Co., 1876), Vol. II, p. 362–363.

16 A.S. Brown, "Missing Links with Mankind in Early Dawn of History," *New York Tribune*, February 10, 1924, p. 11.

17 Ali Gripper, "Blacks Slain for Science's White Superiority Theory," *The Daily Telegraph Mirror*, April 26, 1994, p. 32.

Carl Wieland, "Evolutionary Racism," *Creation*, vol. 20, no. 4, September–November 1998, p. 14–16.

18 Don Richardson, *Eternity in Their Hearts* (Ventura, CA: Regal Books, Division of Gospel Light, 1986).

19 Reed, *Aboriginal Fables and Legendary Tales*, p. 21–22.

20 Hugh Ross, "Genesis One, Dinosaurs, and Cavemen," Reasons to Believe web page, Children's Creation Story, http://www.reasons.org/kidsspace/dinocave.html as of September 29, 1999.

CHAPTER 5

"INTERRACIAL" MARRIAGE?

N ow that we understand that the so-called "races" in reality constitute just one race with different people groups, what about the issue of so-called "interracial marriage?"

If a Chinese person were to marry a Polynesian, or an African with dark skin were to marry a Japanese, or a person from India were to marry a person from America with light skin, would these marriages be in accord with biblical principles?

There are a significant number of Christians (particularly in America) who would claim that such "interracial" marriages violate God's principles in the Bible, and should not be allowed.

But does the Word of God really condemn such mixes as those above? Is there ultimately any such thing as "interracial" marriage?

True science in the present fits with the biblical view that all people are rather closely related — there is only one "race" biologically. Therefore, there is in essence no such thing as "interracial marriage." So we are left with this — is there anything in the Bible that speaks clearly against men and women from different people groups marrying?

ORIGIN OF PEOPLE GROUPS

In Genesis 11, we read of the rebellion at the Tower of Babel that resulted in people being scattered over the earth. Because of this dispersion, and the resulting splitting of the gene pool, different cultures formed, with certain features becoming predominant within each group. Some of these (skin "color," eye shape, and so on) became general characteristics of each particular people group.[1]

Note that the context of Genesis 11 makes it clear that the reason for God's scattering the people over the earth was that they had united in rebellion against God. Some Christians point to this event in an attempt to provide a basis for their arguments against so-called "interracial" marriage. They believe that it is implied here that to keep the nations apart, God is declaring that people from different people groups can't marry. However, there is no such indication in this passage that what is called "interracial marriage" is condemned. Besides, there has been so much mixing of people groups over the years, that it would be impossible for every human being today to trace their lineage to know for certain from which group(s) they are descended.

We need to understand that the sovereign Creator God is in charge of the nations of this world. Paul makes this very clear in Acts 17:26. Some people erroneously claim this verse to mean that people from different nations shouldn't marry. But this passage has nothing to do with marriage. As John Gill makes clear in his classic commentary, the context is that God is in charge of all things — where, how, and for how long any person, tribe, or nation will live, prosper, and perish.[2]

In all of this, God is working to redeem for himself a people who are one in Christ. The Bible makes it clear in Galatians 3:28, Colossians 3:11, and Romans 10:12–13 that in regard to salvation, there is no distinction between male or female or Jew or Greek or bond or free. In Christ, any separation between people is broken down. As Christians, we are one in Christ and thus have a common purpose — to live for Him who made us. This oneness in Christ is vital to understanding marriage.

PURPOSE OF MARRIAGE

Malachi 2:15 declares that an important purpose of marriage is to produce godly offspring — progeny that are trained in the ways of the Lord Jesus in Matthew 19. Also, Paul, in Ephesians 5, makes it clear that when a man and woman marry, they become one flesh (because they were one flesh historically — Eve was made from Adam). In addition, the man and woman must be one spiritually so they can fulfill the command to produce godly offspring. This is why Paul states in 2 Corinthians 6:14, "Do not be unequally yoked together with unbelievers; for what fellowship does righteousness have with lawlessness? And what partnership does light have with darkness?"

According to the Bible then, which of the impending marriages in the illustration on the following page does God counsel against entering into?

The answer is obvious — the third one. According to the Bible, the priority in marriage is that a Christian should marry only a Christian.

Sadly, there are some Christian homes where the parents are more concerned about their children not marrying someone from another "race" than whether or not they are marrying a Christian. When Christians marry non-Christians, it negates the spiritual (not the physical) oneness in marriage, resulting in negative consequences for the couple and their children.

It is true that in some exceptional instances when a Christian has married a non-Christian, the non-Christian spouse, by the grace of God, has become a Christian. This is a praise point, but it does not negate the fact that Scripture indicates that it should not have been entered into in the first place. This does not mean that the marriage is not actually valid, nor does it dilute the responsibilities of the marital union — see also 1 Corinthians 7:12–14, where the context is of one partner becoming a Christian after marriage.

RAHAB AND RUTH

The examples of Rahab and Ruth help us understand how God views the issue of marriage between those who are from different people groups but trust in the true God.

Rahab was a Canaanite. She came from an ungodly culture — descendants of Canaan, the son of Ham. Remember that Canaan was cursed because of his obvious rebellious nature. Unfortunately, many Christians state that Ham was cursed, but this is not true (see Gen. 9:18–27). Some have even said that this non-existent curse of Ham resulted in the black "races." This is absurd and is the type of false teaching that has reinforced and justified prejudices against people with dark skin (see chapter 6).

In the genealogy in Matthew 1, it is traditionally understood that the same Rahab is listed here as being in the line leading to Christ. Thus Rahab, a descendant of Ham, must have married an Israelite (descended from Shem). Since this was clearly a union approved by God, it underlines the fact that the particular "people group" she came from was irrelevant — what mattered was that she trusted in the true God of the Israelites.

The same can be said of Ruth, who, as a Moabitess, also married an Israelite, and is also listed in the genealogy in Matthew 1 that leads to Christ. Prior to her marriage to Boaz, she had expressed faith in the true God (Ruth 1:16). It is true that the Israelites were told by God not to marry people from surrounding nations (Lev. 18), but this was because these were pagan peoples, and marriages with them would destroy God's purpose for this sacred institution.

When Rahab and Ruth became children of God, there was no longer any barrier to Israelites marrying them, even though they were from different "people groups."

REAL BIBLICAL "INTERRACIAL" MARRIAGE

If one wants to use the term "interracial," then the real "interracial" marriage that God says we should not enter into is when a child of the Last Adam (one who is a new creation in Christ — a Christian) marries one who is an unconverted child of the First Adam (one who is dead in trespasses and sin — a non-Christian).

These are the two "races" of humans that should not intermarry. Examples of such "mixed marriages" and their negative consequences can be seen in Nehemiah 9 and 10, and Numbers 25.

The family is the first and most fundamental of all human institutions. It is the unit that God uses to transmit His Word from one generation to the next. In Malachi 2:15, when the prophet asked the question, "Why did God make two one?" (alluding to the account of the creation of the first man and woman — the first marriage), the answer was given that God sought a godly seed (godly offspring).

> And did He not make you one? Yet the vestige of the Spirit is in him. And what of the one? He was seeking a godly seed. Then guard your spirit, and do not act treacherously with the wife of your youth (Mal. 2:15).

In other words, it is of primary importance in marriage to produce *godly* offspring, who themselves will then produce godly offspring, generation after generation. Satan knows that if this can be stopped, then the generations to come will not have the knowledge of the Lord.

One of the best ways to destroy the family and its function of producing *godly* offspring, is to have godly people marry ungodly mates. It is obvious that Satan has attempted to do this right down through history. The Israelites often disobeyed God's commandments and married those from pagan cultures who then

THE REAL BIBLICAL INTERRACIAL MARRIAGE

For as in Adam all die, even so in Christ shall all be made alive.
1 Corinthians 15:22

When a child of the LAST ADAM

marries a child of the FIRST ADAM

brought their pagan religion into the Israelite culture. This destroyed the purpose of the family.

From Numbers 31 and 25, we find that Balaam counseled the enemies of Israel on how to destroy God's people. They were to get the Israelite men to marry the women from their pagan culture. Balaam knew that by destroying the godly family, one could ultimately destroy a nation which trusted in God.

> Behold, these caused the sons of Israel, through the counsel of Balaam, to commit sin against the Lord in the matter of Peor, and the plague was on the congregation of the Lord (Num. 31:16).

> And Israel lived in Shittim, and the people began to fornicate with the daughters of Moab. And they called the people to the sacrifices of their gods. And the people ate and bowed down to their gods (Num. 25:1–2).

Today, just like the Israelites, many Christian young people date and marry non-Christians, thus destroying the meaning of the family. Parents need to be diligent in teaching their children the true biblical principles of marriage. Sadly, this is not done in many Christian homes. Instead, often non-biblical ideas that engender racial prejudice are imposed on these offspring.

CROSS-CULTURAL PROBLEMS

Because many people groups have been separated since the Tower of Babel, they have developed many cultural differences. If two people from very different cultures marry, they can have a number of communication problems, even if both are Christians. Expectations regarding relationships with members of the extended family, for example, can also differ. Even people from different English-speaking countries can have communication problems because words may have different meanings. Counselors should go through this in detail, anticipating the problems and giving specific examples. Some marriages have failed because of such cultural differences. However, such problems have nothing to do with genetics or "race." And ultimately, if a couple are one spiritually, and believe before the Lord that they should be joined in marriage, there is nothing in the Bible that speaks against this union.

In summary then:

1. There is no biblical justification for claiming that people from different so-called "races" (best described as "people groups") should not marry.

2. The biblical basis for marriage makes it clear that a Christian should *only* marry a Christian.

When Christians legalistically impose non-biblical ideas such as "no interracial marriage" onto their culture, they are helping to perpetuate prejudices that have often arisen from evolutionary influences. If we are really honest, in countries like America, the main reason for Christians being against "interracial marriage" is, in most instances, really because of skin "color." (As we have shown, every human being has the same skin color — it just depends on how much of the color one has.)

The Christian Church could greatly relieve the tensions over racism if only the leaders would teach that all people are descended from one man and woman, and all people are equal before God. Furthermore, all are sinners in need of salvation; all need to build their thinking on God's Word and judge all their cultural aspects accordingly; all need to be one in Christ, and put an end to their rebellion against their Creator.

ENDNOTES

1 Don Batten, Ken Ham, Jonathan Sarfati, Andrew Snelling, Carl Wieland, "How Did All the Different 'Races' Arise (from Noah's Family)?" *The Answers Book*, (Green Forest, AR: Master Books, Inc., 1999 revision), chapter 18.

   "Rugby Star Proof of Evolution," *Creation*, vol. 18, no. 1, December 1995–February 1996, p. 8.

   "Races Very Close," *Creation*, vol. 17, no. 2, March–May 1995, p. 9.

   "Modern 'Stone Age' Reconsidered," *Creation*, vol. 15, no. 4, September–November 1993, p. 51.

   Carl Wieland, "Shades of Babel," *Creation*, vol. 13, no. 1, December 1990–February 1991, p. 23.

   Dennis and Lyn Field (translators), "Julmbanu: Aboriginal Babel," *Creation*, vol. 8, no. 2, March 1986, p. 11.

   Jerry Bergman, "Evolution and the Origins of the Biological Race Theory," *CEN Technical Journal*, vol. 7, no. 2, 1993, p. 155–168.

2 See note on Acts 17:26 in: John Gill, *An Exposition of the Old and New Testament; The Whole Illustrated with Notes, Taken from the Most Ancient Jewish Writings* (London: printed for Mathews and Leigh, 18 Strand, by W. Clowes, Northumberland-Court, 1809), nine volumes, edited, revised, and updated by Larry Pierce, 1994–1995, for the *Online Bible* CD-ROM.

CHAPTER 6

ARE BLACK PEOPLE THE RESULT OF A CURSE ON HAM?

It has been clearly shown that the blackness of, for example, "black" Africans is merely one particular combination of inherited factors. This means that these factors themselves, though not in that combination, were originally present in Adam and Eve. The belief that the skin color of black people is a result of a curse on Ham and his descendants *is taught nowhere in the Bible*. Furthermore, it was not Ham who was cursed; it was his son, Canaan (Gen. 9:18, 25; 10:6), and Canaan's descendants were probably brown-skinned (Gen. 10:15–19).

The following two quotes illustrate how people

have been falsely misled concerning Ham and Canaan. In 1958, from the writings of the Mormon Church:

> We know the circumstances under which the posterity of Cain (and later of Ham) were cursed with what we call Negroid racial characteristics.[1]

In 1929, a Jehovah's Witness publication stated:

> The curse which Noah pronounced upon Canaan was the origin of the black race.[2]

False teaching about Ham has been used to justify slavery and other non-biblical, racist attitudes. It is traditionally believed that the African nations are largely Hamitic, because the Cushites (Cush was a son of Ham — Gen. 10:6) are thought to have lived where Ethiopia is today. Genesis suggests that the dispersion was probably along family lines, and it may be that Ham's descendants were on average darker than, say, Japheth's. However, it could just as easily have been the other way around.

Let's consider some of the details surrounding the curse on Canaan. In Genesis 9:18–27 we read:

> And the sons of Noah that went out of the ark were Shem, Ham, and Japheth. And Ham is the father of Canaan. These are the three sons of Noah, and the whole earth was overspread from them. And Noah began to be a husbandman. And he planted a vineyard. And he drank of the wine and was drunk. And he was uncovered inside his tent. And Ham,

the father of Canaan, saw the nakedness of his father, and told his two brothers outside. And Shem and Japheth took a garment and laid it upon both their shoulders. And they went backwards and covered the nakedness of their father. And their faces were backwards, and they did not see their father's nakedness. And Noah awoke from his wine, and came to know what his younger son had done to him. And he said, Cursed be Canaan. He shall be a servant of servants to his brothers. And he said, Blessed be the Lord God of Shem, and Canaan shall be his servant. God shall enlarge Japheth, and he shall dwell in the tents of Shem. And Canaan shall be their servant.

Notice that when the sons of Noah are listed, Ham is described as being "the father of Canaan." The names of the other two sons are mentioned, but Ham is particularly singled out as being the father of Canaan. Why is this so?

Now Ham had four sons, Cush, Mizraim, Phut, and Canaan. However, consider the descendants of Canaan.

The descendants of Canaan were some of the most wicked people to ever live on the earth — the people of Sodom and Gomorrah for instance. What is interesting to note is that the Bible seems to indicate, in Genesis 9:22, that when Ham was disrespectful to his father, Noah, this involved some sort of sexual connotation.

It is indeed possible that Noah saw in Canaan the

same sin problem that his father Ham had. It is a sad fact of history (there are a number of recorded instances in the Bible) that when the father sins, the next generation learn from the father and are often more wicked than their father.

Therefore, it seems that Noah understood that Canaan's descendants would also reflect this rebellious nature. Remember, the people of Sodom and Gomorrah

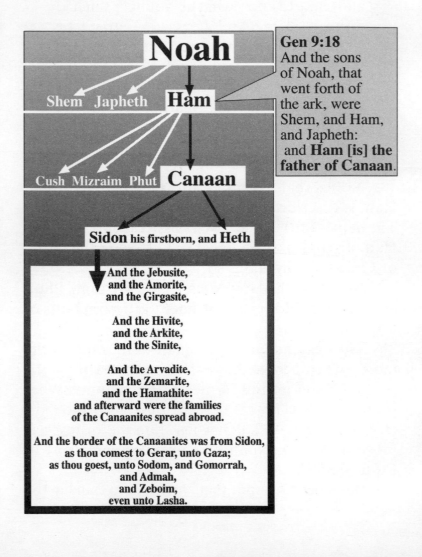

Noah

Shem Japheth **Ham**

Cush Mizraim Phut **Canaan**

Gen 9:18 And the sons of Noah, that went forth of the ark, were Shem, and Ham, and Japheth: and **Ham [is] the father of Canaan**.

Sidon his firstborn, and **Heth**

And the Jebusite, and the Amorite, and the Girgasite,

And the Hivite, and the Arkite, and the Sinite,

And the Arvadite, and the Zemarite, and the Hamathite: and afterward were the families of the Canaanites spread abroad.

And the border of the Canaanites was from Sidon, as thou comest to Gerar, unto Gaza; as thou goest, unto Sodom, and Gomorrah, and Admah, and Zeboim, even unto Lasha.

were judged for their sexual perversion.

The curse of Canaan has nothing whatsoever to do with skin color, but is in fact an example warning fathers to train their children in godly principles. If this is not done in one generation, then generations to come will express their rebellious nature as seen in the wickedness of Canaan's descendants.

ENDNOTES

1 Bruce McConkie, "Apostle of the Mormon Council of 12," *Mormon Doctrine*, 1958, p. 554.

2 "The Golden Age," *The Watchtower* (now is called *Awake!*), July 24, 1929: 702.

CHAPTER 7

PSEUDO-BIBLICAL ARGUMENTS REFUTED

I t should be clear by now that the Bible contains no prohibition against "interracial marriages." This contrasts with the clear biblical arguments against Christians marrying non-Christians, as well as against "homosexual marriages" (a contradiction in terms), despite some groups committing the "guilt by association" fallacy in linking these to interracial marriages. Some people, however, have advanced a number of supposedly scriptural justifications for prohibiting interracial marriages.

IT WILL LEAD TO "ONE-WORLD GOVERNMENT"

Some Christian leaders claim that "interracial marriage" should not be allowed because it will help usher in a one-world government. The argument goes something like this:

> The fact that God made at least three distinct racial strains on the earth is obvious and indisputable. These "races" are descendants of Noah's three sons: Ham, Shem, and Japheth. Because of this and the dispersion at the Tower of Babel, no attempt should be made to bring the world together [which "interracial marriage" would supposedly accomplish], as this would be in defiance of God's plan for the nations to be separate. Such an act of rebellion is a result of man wanting to rule the world apart from God, and would support a one-world government,[1] economy etc. Certain divisions in the earth were put in place by God to keep the world divided until the Lord comes to bring nations together under His rule. One-worlders promote intermarriage.

But there are a number of major problems and inconsistencies with this view. The most obvious fallacy is that just because one-worlders promote something, it is not proof *in itself* that it is wrong. For example, one-worlders promote healthy diets, and this doesn't mean that healthy diets are wrong. Right and wrong must be decided by Scripture, not by what other people do.

Nowhere in the Bible do we read any statement that even alludes to a prohibition of marriage among the descendants of the three sons of Noah. It is true that in Genesis 9:26–27, Noah did make some prophetic statements about his three sons: "And he said, Blessed be the Lord God of Shem, and Canaan shall be his servant. God shall enlarge Japheth, and he shall dwell in the tents of Shem. And Canaan shall be their servant." And it is true that the descendants of each of these sons have made contributions in accord with Noah's statements.[2] However, it is also true that we are now some 4,500 years since that time and the boundaries between the descendants of each group are very blurred.

We have previously discussed Matthew's genealogy of Christ, through Joseph, Jesus' legal but not biological father (Matt. 1:18–25, Luke 1:34–38). Like all biblical genealogies, Matthew's genealogy was traced through the father's line. But even the S(h)emite Messianic line mentioned three Gentile women — the Hamite women Tamar and Rahab, and the Moabitess (Semitic but non-Jewish) Ruth. Neither Rahab's nor Ruth's ("interracial") marriages with Israelites were in any way condemned by Scripture; rather, they were honored in being named as ancestors of Christ. Matthew's genealogy also listed the Jewess Bathsheba, who had previously been married to the godly Hittite Uriah, a marriage that God severely judged King David for dishonoring.

Now consider the chronology of the events since the flood of Noah. It is likely that the reference to the division of the earth in Peleg's day (Gen. 10:25) refers to the division of languages at Babel. Therefore, a simple addition of the ages of the patriarchs at the birth of their sons (Gen. 11:10–16) shows that Babel must have occurred about 100 years after the flood.

Because there were around 100 years between the

Flood and the Tower of Babel, there was plenty of time for thousands of people to be born before the Babel event. It is, therefore, more than reasonable to assume that the sons and daughters of Ham, Shem, and Japheth married each other. Thus, even though many generations ago one could perhaps trace one's ancestry back to one of the three sons of Noah, for example Japheth, this would not mean that all the descendants were direct from Japheth only, excluding any ancestors from Shem or Ham.

It is true that God divided the people at the time of the Tower of Babel because of their rebellion.

> And the whole earth was of one language and of one speech. And it happened, as they traveled from the east, they found a plain in the land of Shinar. And they lived there. And they said to one another, Come, let us make brick and burn them thoroughly. And they had brick for stone, and they had asphalt for mortar. And they said, Come, let us build us a city and a tower, and its top in the heavens. And let us make a name for ourselves, lest we be scattered upon the face of the whole earth.
>
> And the Lord came down to see the city and the tower which the sons of Adam had built. And the Lord said, Behold! The people is one and they all have one language. And this they begin to do. And now nothing which they have imagined to do will be restrained from them. Come, let Us go down and there confuse their language, so that they cannot

understand one another's speech. So the Lord scattered them abroad from that place upon the face of all the earth. And they quit building the city.

Therefore the name of it is called Babel; because the Lord confused the language of all the earth there. And from there the Lord scattered them abroad on the face of all the earth (Gen. 11:1–9).

Note, however, that the means God used to scatter people over the earth was to "confound their language." Again, there was no mention of marriage, "races," or skin colors here. In fact, if anything was going to bring nations together again, it would be the reversing of the confusion of language. Thus, to be consistent, if some Christians believe nothing should be done that appears to help bring in what they believe would be a one-world government, then such Christians shouldn't study or teach foreign languages (or English-speaking Christians shouldn't teach English to others as a second language).

But the Great Commission tells us:

Therefore go and teach all nations, baptizing them in the name of the Father and of the Son and of the Holy Spirit (Matt. 28:19).

In order to teach all nations, we need to learn their languages so we can communicate with them. There is no doubt that crossing the language barrier has done more to bring the nations together than anything else.

We also must remember that God is in charge of the nations, anyway. Nothing man does is going to thwart the plans God has for the nations for the future. There is a sovereignty issue here. As the Scripture states:

> Behold, the nations are like a drop in a bucket, and are counted as the small dust of the scales (Isa. 40:15).

> O Lord God of our Fathers, are You not God in Heaven? And do You rule over all the kingdoms of the nations? And is there power and might in Your hand, so that none is able to withstand You? (2 Chron. 20:6).

> Remember former things from forever; for I am God, and no other is God, even none like Me, declaring the end from the beginning, and from the past things which were not done, saying, My purpose shall stand, and I will do all My pleasure; calling a bird of prey from the east, the man of my purpose from a far country. Yes, I have spoken, I will also cause it to come; I have formed; yes, I will do it (Isa. 46:9–11).

> When the Most High divided to the nations their inheritance, when He separated the sons of Adam, He set the bounds of the people according to the number of the sons of Israel (Deut. 32:8).

There is no way that anything man does is going to disrupt God's sovereign plans for the nations, whether that be so-called "interracial marriage," learning languages, or whatever.

Another point to consider is that so-called "interracial marriages" between Christians, unlike the disobedience at Babel, would not be helping people to rebel against God. Such marriages would be built upon God's Word, and thus should produce godly offspring (in accordance with the primary importance of marriage — Mal. 2:15 for instance), who would influence the world *for* Christ, not *against* Him (whereas a one-world government referred to by the Christian leaders mentioned above would presumably be one of rebellion against God).

FALSE CLAIM: NON-WHITE "RACES" COME FROM "PRE-ADAMITES"

Often, "Christian" racists are not literal creationists but hold to combinations of the "gap theory" and "pre-Adamites," usually distinguishing the people in Genesis 1 from Adam and Eve in Genesis 2. This provides an excuse to claim that non-whites are not descendants of Adam (although it is Genesis 1 that explicitly says that people were created in the image of God). However, Christ made no such distinction in Matthew 19:3–6 where He cited Genesis 1:27 and 2:24 together, and Paul called Adam the first man in 1 Corinthians 15:45. Some have argued against the latter point by claiming that the word "man" is not in the original Greek. A simple check of a Greek New Testament shows that this claim has no textual support whatever — the Textus Receptus, Majority Text, and Critical Text[3] all have the reading ὁ πρῶτος ἄνθρωπος Αδαμ (*ho pròtos **anthròpos** Adam* = the first **man** Adam).

FALSE CLAIM: ADAM'S NAME MEANS THAT HE MUST HAVE BLUSHED, AND NON-WHITES CAN'T DO THIS

The name of the first man Adam was derived from related Hebrew words meaning "red." Therefore, if Adam's name comes from these word, he must have been able to "go red" or blush, so he must have been "white" because "we know that blacks can't blush." This is blatant eisegesis, i.e., reading a doctrine into the text rather than out of it. This is like a house of cards where each shaky story is built on a shakier story below.

1. Deducing meanings of words from their etymology (derivation), by analyzing common roots, is a very outdated method of Hebrew study. Decades ago, Hebrew scholars termed this sort of analysis "root fallacy."

2. The correct explanation is that the name of the first man Adam was a play on words on the dust or clay (Hebrew *adamah*, אדמה from which he was made. It is the dust which is important in the Genesis account, not similar words meaning "red."

3. Even if we granted that the similarity of his name to words meaning "red" was really significant, then it would surely be more likely to mean that Adam was permanently red, with a complexion more like that of a Native American ("red Indian"), rather than temporarily red due to blushing. It also makes more genetic sense for him to have had a medium-dark complexion, carrying the genes for a wide variety of amounts of melanin, so he could be the ancestor of all people groups with their wide variation in degree of pigmentation.

4. Even if we granted the fanciful story about

blushing, it is not true that dark-skinned people cannot blush. They merely have more of the same pigment that all people groups have, so their blushing is harder to detect visually.

FALSE CLAIM: NON-WHITE PEOPLE ARE THE "BEASTS OF THE FIELD"

Some have claimed that "beasts of the field" mentioned in Genesis actually refers to non-white or "black" people. This is a disgraceful doctrine, and is simply an appeal to prejudice rather than responsible exegesis of the Hebrew, and contradicts the clear teaching that all people are descended from Adam *via* Noah. The Bible says nothing about the amount of melanin in the skin as a criterion either for being a human or for becoming a child of God through faith in Christ (Gal. 3:25–29). After all, Philip ministered to the Ethiopian eunuch (Acts 8:26–40) who was almost certainly very dark-skinned.

ENDNOTES

1 In this book, the authors are not taking a position on eschatology in relation to a future one-world government, but are referring to an argument used by some Christian leaders who associate "interracial marriage" and a one-world government.

2 Henry Morris, *The Genesis Record* (Grand Rapids, MI: Baker Book House, 1976), chapter 9.

3 Arthur L. Farstad et al., translators, *The NKJV Greek English Interlinear* (Nashville, TN: Thomas Nelson, 1994).

CHAPTER 8

"STONE AGE" PEOPLE

A rchaeology shows that there were once people who lived in caves and used simple stone tools. Observation shows that there are still people who do the same. We have seen evidence that all people on earth today are descended from Noah and his family. Before the flood, Genesis indicates there was at least sufficient technology to make musical instruments, to farm, forge metal implements, construct cities, and build a very large seaworthy vessel. After the dispersion at Babel, the hostilities induced by the new languages may have forced some groups to scatter rather rapidly, finding shelter where and when they could.

In some instances, the use of stone tools may simply have been a stage until their settlements were fully established, and they had found and exploited metal deposits, for example. In others, the original diverging group may not have taken all the knowledge with them. Ask an average group today how many of them, if they had to start again, as it were, would know how to find, mine, and smelt metal-bearing rocks (ore bodies). Obviously, there has been technological (cultural) degeneration/loss in many post-Babel groups.

In some cases, harsh environments may have contributed. The Australian Aborigines have a technology and cultural knowledge which, in relation to their lifestyle and need to survive in the dry outback, is most appropriate. This includes aerodynamic principles used in making boomerangs (some of which are designed to return to the thrower, while others are not).

Sometimes we see evidence of degeneration that is hard to explain, but is real, nonetheless. For instance, when Europeans arrived in Tasmania, the Aborigines there had the simplest technology known. They caught no fish, and did not usually make and wear clothes. Yet recent archaeological discoveries lead us to infer that some generations earlier, they had more knowledge and equipment.

For instance, archaeologist Rhys Jones believes that in the Tasmanian Aborigines' distant past, these people had equipment to sew skins into more complex clothes than the skins they just slung over their shoulders, according to all descriptions in the early 1800s. It also appears that they were in fact catching and eating fish in the past, but when Europeans arrived, they had not been doing this for a long time.[1] From this we infer that technology can indeed be lost or abandoned, and is not always retained and built upon.

Animist peoples live in fear of evil spirits and have many taboos against healthy practices like washing themselves and eating various nutritious things, again illustrating how loss of knowledge of the true Creator-God leads to degradation (Rom. 1:18–32).

ENDNOTES

1   Rhys Jones, "Tasmania's Ice-Age Hunters," *Australian Geographic*, no. 8 (October–December 1987), p. 26–45.

R.S.V. Wright, editor, *Stone Tools as Cultural Markers,* "The Tasmanian Paradox" by Rhys Jones (Canberra, Australia: Australian Institute of Aboriginal Studies, 1977).

CHAPTER 9

DARWIN'S BODY SNATCHERS

A gruesome trade in "missing link" specimens began with early evolutionary/racist ideas. But this trade really "took off" with the advent of Darwinism.[1]

There is documented evidence that the remains of perhaps 10,000 of Australia's Aboriginal people were shipped to British museums in a frenzied attempt to prove the widespread belief that they were the "missing link."[2] A major item in a leading Australian weekly, *The Bulletin*, revealed other shocking new facts. Some of the points covered in the article, written by Australian journalist David Monaghan, make up much of this chapter.

Evolutionists in the United States were also strongly involved in this flourishing "industry" of gathering specimens of "sub-humans." The Smithsonian Institution in Washington holds the remains of 15,000 individuals of various races.

Along with museum curators from around the world, Monaghan says, some of the top names in British science were involved in this large-scale grave-robbing trade. These included anatomist Sir Richard Owen, anthropologist Sir Arthur Keith, and Charles Darwin himself. Darwin wrote asking for Tasmanian skulls when only four of the island's Aborigines were left alive, provided his request would not "upset" their feelings. Museums were not only interested in bones, but in fresh skins as well. These would provide interesting evolutionary displays when stuffed.[3]

Pickled Aboriginal brains were also in demand to try to prove that they were inferior to those of whites. It was Darwin, after all, who wrote that the civilized races would inevitably wipe out such lesser-evolved "savage" ones.

Good prices were being offered for such specimens. There is no doubt from written evidence that many of the "fresh" specimens were obtained by simply going out and killing the Aboriginal people. The way in which the requests for specimens were announced was often a poorly disguised invitation to do just that. A death-bed memoir from Korah Wills, who became mayor of Bowen, Queensland, in 1866,[4] graphically describes how he killed and dismembered a local tribesman in 1865 to provide a scientific specimen.[5]

Edward Ramsay, curator of the Australian Museum in Sydney for 20 years starting in 1874, was particularly heavily involved. He published a museum booklet, which appeared to include Aborigines under the designation of "Australian animals." It also gave instructions not only on how to rob graves, but also on

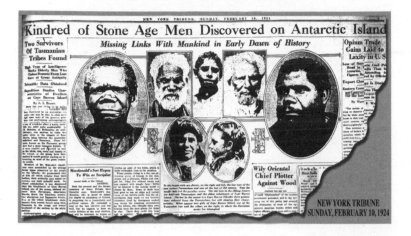

NEW YORK TRIBUNE
SUNDAY, FEBRUARY 10, 1924

how to plug up bullet wounds in freshly killed "specimens." Many freelance collectors worked under his guidance. Four weeks after he had requested skulls of Bungee (Russell River) blacks, a keen young science student sent him two, announcing that they, the last of their tribe, had just been shot.[6] In the 1880s, Ramsay complained that laws recently passed in Queensland to stop Aborigines being slaughtered were affecting his supply.

ANGEL OF BLACK DEATH

A German evolutionist, Amalie Dietrich (nicknamed the "Angel of Black Death") came to Australia asking station ("ranch") owners for Aborigines to be shot for specimens, particularly skin for stuffing and mounting for her museum employers.[7] Although evicted from at least one property, she shortly returned home with her specimens.

A New South Wales missionary was a horrified witness to the slaughter by mounted police of a group of dozens of Aboriginal men, women, and children.[8] Forty-five heads were then boiled down and the 10 best skulls were packed off for overseas.

Darwinist views about the racial inferiority of Aborigines (backed up by biased distortions of the evidence since shown to be false) drastically influenced their treatment. In 1908 an inspector from the Department of Aborigines in the West Kimberley region wrote that he was glad to have received an order to transport all half-castes away from their tribe to the mission. He said it was "the duty of the State" to give these children (who, by evolutionary reasoning, were going to be intellectually superior) a "chance to lead a better life than their mothers." He wrote, "I would not hesitate for one moment to separate a half-caste from an Aboriginal mother, no matter how frantic her momentary grief."[9]

Such separation policies continued until the 1960s.

The demand has not entirely abated. Aboriginal bones have still been sought by major institutions in quite modern times.

MEN OF ONE BLOOD

And where was the Church in all this? It was much more influential back then, but it had already begun to be influenced itself by the "new thinking" about origins and was not prepared to take a stand on creation issues. However, the apostle Paul's ringing declaration, backed up by the facts of human history revealed in Genesis, was that God had "made all men of one blood" (Acts 17:26). This is now reinforced by modern biology as well.

The issue of these pilfered remains is becoming politically sensitive in Australia. There is now much pressure from Aboriginal leaders and others for the remains to be returned.

Aboriginal rage at this desecration of their ancestors would also be appropriately directed at the anti-biblical thought patterns of evolution responsible for this outrage.

This phenomenon of mild-mannered museum officials, respected scientists, and mayors, for example, casually going about their daily respectable lives while they were involved in monstrous acts justified by a scientific doctrine, was unparalleled in history to that point.

A similar horror reappeared in the 1930s, when the blatantly evolutionary doctrines of Nazism allowed the consciences of hundreds of doctors, scientists, psychiatrists, and other officials to be seared as they set up the machinery to help nature eliminate the unfit. First, it was the genetically "inferior" — the mentally and physically disabled. Next, gypsies, Jews, and others. The rest of the story is well known.

Today, evolutionary thinking enables ordinary, respectable professionals, otherwise dedicated to the saving of life, to justify their involvement in the slaughter of millions of unborn human beings, who, like the Aborigines of earlier Darwinian thinking, are also deemed "not yet fully human."

ENDNOTES

1 Originally published in *Creation*, vol. 14, no. 2, March–May 1992, p. 16-18.

2 "Darwin's Body Snatchers," *Creation*, vol. 12, no. 3, June–August 1990, p. 21.

3 David Monaghan, "The Body-Snatchers," *The Bulletin*, November 12, 1991, p. 30–38. (The article states that journalist Monaghan spent 18 months researching this subject in London, culminating in a television documentary called

Darwin's Body-Snatchers, which was aired in Britain on
October 8, 1990.)

4   According to the records of the Bowen Shire Council.

5   Monaghan, "The Body-Snatchers," p. 33. In this article,
Monaghan quotes two long paragraphs from Korah
Will's five-page manuscript.

6   Ibid., p. 34. Monaghan identifies the student as W.S. Day.

7   Ibid., p. 33. Monaghan is here quoting Dr. Rae Sumner, a
lecturer at the Queensland Institute of Technology's
School of Language and Literacy Education.

8   Ibid., p. 34. Monaghan identifies the missionary as
Lancelot Threlkeld.

9   Ibid., p. 38.

CHAPTER 10

OTA BENGA: THE PYGMY PUT ON DISPLAY IN A ZOO

O ne of the most fascinating historical accounts about the effects of Darwinism is
the story of Ota Benga, a Pygmy who was
put on display in an American zoo as an example of
an inferior race.[1] The incident clearly reveals the racism of Darwinism and the extent to which the theory
gripped the hearts and minds of scientists and jour-
nalists in the early 1900s. As humans move away from
this time in history, we can more objectively look
back at the horrors that Darwinism has brought to
society, of which this story is one poignant example.

Genetic differences are crucial to the theory of

Darwinism because they are the only ultimate source of the innovation required for evolution. History and tradition have, often with tragic consequences, grouped human phenotypes that result from genotypic variations together into categories now called "races." Races function as evolutionary selection units of such importance that the subtitle of Darwin's classic 1859 book, *The Origin of Species*, was *The Preservation of Favoured Races in the Struggle for Life*. This work was critical in establishing the importance of the race fitness idea, and especially the "survival of the fittest" concept.

The question being asked in the early 1900s was:

> Who was, [and] who wasn't human? It was a big question in turn-of-the-century Europe and America. . . . The Europeans . . . were asking and answering it about Pygmies . . . often influenced by the current interpretations of Darwinism, so it was not simply who was human, but who was more human, and finally, who was the most human, that concerned them.[2]

Darwinism spawned the belief that some races were physically closer to the lower primates and were also inferior. The polyphyletic view was that blacks evolved from the strong but less intelligent gorillas, the Orientals from the Orangutans, and whites from the most intelligent of all primates, the chimpanzees.[3] The belief that blacks were less evolved than whites, and (as many early evolutionists concluded) that they would eventually become extinct, is a major chapter in Darwinism history. The nefarious fruits of evolutionism, from the Nazis' conception of racial superiority to its utilization in developing their governmental policy, are all well documented.[4]

Some scientists felt that the solution to the problem of racism in early 20th-century America was to allow Darwinian natural selection to operate without interference. Bradford and Blume noted that Darwin taught:

> . . . when left to itself, natural selection would accomplish extinction. Without slavery to embrace and protect them, or so it was thought, blacks would have to compete with Caucasians for survival. Whites' greater fitness for this contest was [they believed] beyond dispute. The disappearance of blacks as a race, then, would only be a matter of time.[5]

Each new American census showed that this prediction of Darwin was wrong because "the black population showed no signs of failing, and might even be on the rise." Not content "to wait for natural selection to grind out the answer," one senator even tried to establish programs to convince — or even force — Afro-Americans to return to Africa.[6]

One of the more poignant incidents in the history of Darwinism and racism is the story of the man put on display in a zoo.[7] Brought from the Belgian Congo in 1904 by noted African explorer Samuel Verner, he was eventually "presented by Verner to the Bronx Zoo director, William Hornaday."[8] The man, a Pygmy named Ota Benga (or "Bi" which means "friend" in Benga's language), was born in 1881 in central Africa.

When placed in the zoo, although about 23 years old, he was only four-feet eleven-inches tall and weighed a mere 103 pounds. Often referred to as a boy, he was actually a twice-married father — his first wife and two children were murdered by the white colonists, and his second spouse died from a poisonous snake bite.[9]

Ota was first displayed as an "emblematic savage" in the anthropology wing at the 1904 St. Louis World's Fair with other Pygmies. The exhibit was under the direction of W.J. McGee of the St. Louis World's Fair Anthropology Department. McGee's ambition for the exhibit was to "be exhaustively scientific" in his demonstration of the stages of human evolution. Therefore he required "darkest blacks" to set off against "dominant whites" and members of the "lowest known culture" to contrast with "its highest culmination."[10] Ironically, Professor Franz Boas of Columbia University "lent his name" to the anthropological exhibit. This was ironic because Boas, a Jew who was one of the first anthropologists who opposed the racism of Darwinism, spent his life fighting the now infamous eugenics movement.[11]

The extremely popular exhibit attracted "considerable attention."[12] Pygmies were selected because they had attracted much attention as an example of a primitive race. One *Scientific American* article said:

> The personal appearance, characteristics, and traits of the Congo Pygmies . . . [they are] small, ape-like, elfish creatures, furtive and mischievous . . . [who] live in the dense tangled forests in absolute savagery, and while

they exhibit many ape-like features in their bodies, they possess a certain alertness, which appears to make them more intelligent than other negroes. . . .

The existence of the Pygmies is of the rudest; they do not practice agriculture, and keep no domestic animals. They live by means of hunting and snaring, eking this out by means of thieving from the big negroes, on the outskirts of whose tribes they usually establish their little colonies, though they are as unstable as water, and range far and wide through the forests. They have seemingly become acquainted with metal only through contact with superior beings.[13]

During the Pygmies' stay in America, they were studied by scientists to learn how the "barbaric races" compared with intellectually defective Caucasians on intelligence tests, and how they responded to such things as pain.[14] The anthropometricians and psychometricians concluded that intelligence tests proved that Pygmies were similar to "mentally deficient persons, making many stupid errors and taking an enormous amount of time."[15] Many Darwinists put the Pygmies' level of evolution "squarely in the Paleolithic period" and Gatti concluded they had the "cruelty of the primitive man."[16] Nor did they do very well in sports. In Bradford and Blume's words, "The disgraceful record set by the ignoble savages" was so poor that "never before in the history of sport . . . were such poor performances recorded."[17]

The anthropologists then measured not only the

live humans, but in one case a "primitive's head was severed from the body and boiled down to the skull." Believing skull size was an "index of intelligence, scientists were amazed" to discover the "primitive's" skull was "larger than that which had belonged to the statesman Daniel Webster."[18]

A *Scientific American* editor concluded:

> Of the native tribes to be seen in the exposition, the most primitive are the Negritos. ... nothing makes them so happy as to show their skill, by knocking a five-cent piece out of a twig of a tree at a distance of fifteen paces. Then there is the village of the Head-Hunting Igorotes, a race that is . . . a fine type of agricultural barbarians.[19]

The same source referred to Pygmies as "ape-like little black people" and theorized that the evolution of the anthropoid apes was soon followed by:

> ... the earliest type of humanity which entered the Dark Continent, and these too, urged on by the pressure of superior tribes, were gradually forced into the great forests. The human type, in all probability, first emerged from the ape in southeastern Asia, possibly in India. The higher types forced the Negro from the continent in an eastward direction, across the intervening islands, as far as Australia, and westward into Africa. Even today, ape-like Negroes are found in the gloomy forests, who are doubtless direct de-

scendants of these early types of man, who probably closely resembled their simian ancestors. . . .

They are often dirty-yellowish brown in color and covered with a fine down. Their faces are fairly hairy, with great prognathism, and retreating chins, while in general they are unintelligent and timid, having little tribal cohesion and usually living upon the fringes of higher tribes. Among the latter, individual types of the lower order crop out now and then, indicating that the two were, to a certain extent merged in past ages.[20]

While on display, the Pygmies were treated in marked contrast to how they first treated the whites who came to Africa to see them. When Verner visited the African king, "he was met with songs and presents, food and palm wine, drums. He was carried in a hammock." In contrast, when the Batwa were in St. Louis they were treated, "With laughter. Stares. People came to take their picture and run away . . . [and] came to fight with them. . . . Verner had contracted to bring the Pygmies safely back to Africa. It was often a struggle just to keep them from being torn to pieces at the fair. Repeatedly . . . the crowds became agitated and ugly; the pushing and grabbing took on a frenzied quality. Each time, Ota and the Batwa were "extracted only with difficulty." Frequently, the police were summoned.[21]

HOW OTA CAME TO THE UNITED STATES

Ota Benga was spared from a massacre perpetuated by the Force Publique, a group of thugs working for the Belgium government endeavoring to extract tribute (in other words, steal labor and raw materials) from the native Africans in the Belgian Congo. After Ota successfully killed an elephant on a hunt, he returned to his people with the good news. Tragically the camp Ota had left behind had ceased to exist — his wife and children were all murdered, and their bodies were mutilated in a campaign of terror undertaken by the Belgian government against the "evolutionarily inferior natives."[22] Ota was himself later captured, brought to a village, and sold into slavery.

In the meantime, Verner was looking for several Pygmies to display at the Louisiana Purchase exposition and spotted Ota at a slave market. Verner bent down,

> . . . and pulled the Pygmy's lips apart to examine his teeth. He was elated; the filed [to sharp points] teeth proved the little man was one of those he was commissioned to bring back. . . . With salt and cloth he was buying him for freedom, Darwinism, and the West.[23]

Ota's world was shattered by the whites, and although he did not know if the white man who was now his master had the same intentions as the Belgians, he knew he had little choice but to go with Verner. Besides this, the events of the slave market were only one more event in Ota's life which pushed him further into the nightmare which began with his discovery of the slaughter and gross mutilation of his family.

Verner managed to coerce only four Pygmies to

go back with him, a number which "fell far short of McGee's initial specification," because "the shopping list . . . called for eighteen Africans, but it would do."[24]

After the fair, Verner took Ota and the other Pygmies back to Africa — Ota almost immediately remarried, but his second wife soon died. He now no longer belonged to any clan or family since they were all killed or sold into slavery. The rest of his people also ostracized him, called him a warlock, and claimed that he had chosen to stand in the white man's world outside of theirs.

The white men were simultaneously admired and feared, and were regarded with both awe and concern: they could do things like record human voices on Edison cylinder phonographs, which the Pygmies saw as something that stole the "soul" from the body, allowing the body to sit and listen to its soul talking.[25]

While back in Africa, Verner collected artifacts for his museums. He then decided to take Ota back to America (although Verner claimed that it was Ota's idea) for a visit — Verner would return him to Africa on his next trip.

Once back in America, Verner tried to sell his animals to zoos, and sell the crates of artifacts that he had brought back from Africa to museums. Verner was by then having serious money problems and could not afford to take care of Ota, so he needed to place him somewhere. When Ota was presented to Director Hornaday of the Bronx Zoological Gardens, Hornaday's intention was clearly to "display" Ota. Hornaday "maintained the hierarchical view of races . . . large-brained animals were to him what Nordics were to Grant, the best evolution had to offer."[26] A "believer in the Darwinian theory" he also concluded that there exists "a close analogy of the African savage to the apes."[27]

At first Ota was free to wander around the zoo, helping out with the animals, but this was soon to drastically change.

> Hornaday and other zoo officials had long been subject to a recurring dream in which a man like Ota Benga played a leading role . . . a trap was being prepared, made of Darwinism, Barnumism, pure and simple racism . . . so seamlessly did these elements come together that later those responsible could deny, with some plausibility, that there had ever been a trap or plan at all. There was no one to blame, they argued, unless it was a capricious Pygmy or a self-serving press.[28]

Ota was next encouraged to spend more time inside the monkey house. He was even given a bow and arrow and was encouraged to shoot it as part of "an exhibit." Ota was soon locked in his enclosure — and when he was let out of the monkey house, "the crowd stayed glued to him, and a keeper stayed close by."[29] In the meantime, the publicity began on September 9, a *New York Times* headline screamed "Bushman shares a cage with Bronx Park apes." Although director Dr. Hornaday insisted that he was merely offering an "intriguing exhibit" for the public's edification:

> [He] . . . apparently saw no difference between a wild beast and the little black man; [and] for the first time in any American zoo,

a human being was displayed in a cage. Benga was given cage-mates to keep him company in his captivity — a parrot and an orangutan named Dohong.[30]

A contemporary account stated that Ota was "not much taller than the orangutan . . . their heads are much alike, and both grin in the same way when pleased."[31] Benga also came over from Africa with a "fine young chimpanzee" which Mr. Verner also deposited "in the ape collection at the Primates House."[32] Hornaday's enthusiasm for his new primate exhibit was reflected in an article that he wrote for the zoological society's bulletin, which begins as follows:

> On September 9, a *genuine* African Pygmy, belonging to the sub-race commonly miscalled "the dwarfs." . . . Ota Benga is a well-developed little man, with a good head, bright eyes, and a pleasing countenance. He is not hairy, and is not covered by the "downy fell" described by some explorers. . . . He is happiest when at work, making something with his hands (emphasis in original).

Hornaday then tells how he obtained the Pygmy from Verner who,

> . . . was specially interested in the Pygmies, having recently returned to their homes on the Kasai River the half dozen men and women of that race who were brought to this country by him for exhibition in the

Department of Anthropology at the St.
Louis [World's Fair] Exposition.[33]

THE INFLUENCE OF EVOLUTION

The many factors motivating Verner to bring Ota
to the United States were complex, but he was evidently "much influenced by the theories of Charles
Darwin," a theory which, as it developed, increasingly divided humankind up into arbitrarily con-
trived "races."[34] Verner also believed that the blacks
were an "inferior race."[35] As Hallet shows, Darwin
also felt that the Pygmies were inferior humans:

> The Darwinian dogma of slow and
> gradual evolution from brutish ancestors .
> . . contributed to the pseudohistory of man-
> kind. On the last page of his book *The De-
> scent of Man*, Darwin expressed the opin-
> ion that he would rather be descended from
> a monkey than from a "savage." He used
> the words savage, low, and degraded to de-
> scribe the American Indians, the Andaman
> Island Pygmies, and the representatives of
> almost every ethnic group whose physical
> appearance and culture differed from his
> own. . . . [In this way] Charles Darwin la-
> beled "the low and degraded inhabitants of
> the Andaman Islands" in his book *The De-
> scent of Man*. The Iruri Forest Pygmies have
> been compared to "lower organisms."[36]

Although biological racism did not begin with Darwinism, Darwin did more than any other person to

popularize it. As early as 1699, English physician Edward Tyson studied a skeleton which he believed belonged to a Pygmy, concluding that Pygmies were apes. It later turned out that the skeleton on which this conclusion was based was actually a chimpanzee.[37]

The conclusion accepted by most scientists in Verner's day was that after Darwin "showed that all humans descended from apes" he proved "that some races had descended farther than others . . . [and that] some races, namely the white ones, had left the ape far behind, while other races, Pygmies especially, had hardly matured at all."[38] Many scientists agreed with scholar Sir Harry Johnson who studied the Pygmies and concluded that they were "very apelike in appearance [and] their hairy skins, the length of their arms, the strength of their thickset frames, their furtive ways, their arboreal habits all point to these people as representing man in one of his earlier forms."[39]

One of the most extensive early studies of the Pygmies concluded that they were "queer little freaks. . . . The low state of their mental development is shown by the following facts. They have no regard for time, nor have they any records or traditions of the past; no religion is known among them, nor have they any fetish rights; they do not seek to know the future by occult means . . . in short, they are . . . the closest link with the original Darwinian anthropoid ape extant."[40]

The Pygmies were in fact a talented group — experts at mimicry, physically agile, quick, nimble, and superior hunters, but the Darwinists did not look for these traits because they were blinded by their "evolution glasses."[41] Modern study has shown the Pygmies in a far more accurate light and demonstrates how absurd the 1900s evolutionary worldview actually was.[42]

Ota Benga was referred to by C.F. Jayne as "a bright little man"[43] who taught her how to make a set of "string figures" that made up one chapter in her book on the subject. Construction of string figures is a lost folk art at which Ota excelled. Hallet, in defense of Pygmies noted:

> Darwin theorized that primitive people — or "savages," as he called them — do not and cannot envision a universal and benevolent creator. Schebesta's excellent study . . . correctly explains that the religion of the Ituri Forest Pygmies is founded on the belief that "God possesses the totality of vital force, of which he distributes a part to his creatures, an act by which he brings them into existence or perfects them."
>
> Scientists still accept or endorse the theory of religious evolution propounded by Darwin and his nineteenth-century colleagues. They maintained that religion evolved from primitive animism to fetishism to polytheism to the heights of civilized Judeo-Christian monotheism. The Ituri Forest Pygmies are the most primitive living members of our species, yet far from being animistic, they pooh-pooh the local Negro tribes' fears of evil spirits. "If darkness is, darkness is good," according to a favorite Pygmy saying. "He who made the light also makes the darkness." The Pygmies deplore as superstitious nonsense the Negroes'

magico-religious figurines and other so-called fetishes. They would take an equally dim view of churchly huts adorned with doll-like statues of Jesus and Mary. This would be regarded as idol worship by the Ituri Forest Pygmies, who believe that the divine power of the universe cannot be confined within material bounds. The authors of the Hebrew Old Testament would certainly agree, since they observed the well-known commandment forbidding "graven images" or idols.[44]

Verner was no uninformed academic, but "compiled an academic record unprecedented at the University of South Carolina," and in 1892 graduated first in his class at the age of 19 years. In his studies, Verner familiarized himself with the works of Charles Darwin. *The Origin of Species* and *The Descent of Man* engaged Verner on an intellectual level, as the theory of evolution promised to give scientific precision to racial questions that had long disturbed him. According to Darwin . . . it was "more probable that our early progenitors lived on the African continent than elsewhere."[45]

His studies motivated him to look for answers to questions about Pygmies such as:

Are they men, or the highest apes? Who and what were their ancestors? What are their ethnic relations to the other races of men? Have they degenerated from larger men, or are the larger men a development of Pygmy forefathers? These questions arise naturally, and plunge the inquirer at once into the depths of the most heated scientific discussions of this generation.[46]

One hypothesis that he considered was:

> Pygmies present a case of unmodified structure from the beginning [a view which is] . . . against both evolution and degeneracy. It is true that these little people have apparently preserved an unchanged physical entity for five thousand years. But that only carries the question back into the debated ground of the origin of species. The point at issue is distinct. Did the Pygmies come from a man who was a common ancestor to many races now as far removed from one another as my friend Teku of the Batwa village is from the late President McKinley?[47]

Many people saw a clear conflict between evolution and Christianity, and "for most men, the moral resolve of an evangelist like Livingstone and the naturalism of a Darwin canceled each other out." To Verner, though, no contradiction existed: he was "equally drawn to evangelism and evolutionism, Livingstone, and Darwin." In short, the "huge gap between religion and science" did not concern Verner. He soon went to Africa to "satisfy his curiosity first hand about questions of natural history and human evolution."[48] He later wrote much about his trips to Africa, even advocating that whites take over Africa and run the country as "friendly directors."[49]

Verner concluded that the Pygmies were the "most primitive race of mankind" and were "almost as much at home in the trees as the monkeys."[50] He also argued that the blacks in Africa should be collected into reservations and colonized by "the white race" and that the social and legal conflicts between races should be solved by "local segregation."[51] Verner was not a mean person, and cared deeply for other "races," but this care was influenced in an extremely adverse way by his evolutionary beliefs.[52]

THE ZOO EXHIBIT

Henry Fairfield Osborn, a staunch advocate of evolution who spent much of his life proselytizing his evolutionary faith and attacking those who were critical of evolution, especially William Jennings Bryan, made the opening-day remarks when the zoo exhibit first opened. Osborn and other prominent zoo officials believed that not only was Ota less evolved, but that this exhibit allowed the Nordic race to have "access to the wild in order to recharge itself. The great race, as he sometimes called it, needed a place to turn to now and then where, rifle in hand, it could hone its [primitive] instincts." [53]

The Ota exhibit was described by contemporary accounts as a sensation – the crowds especially loved his gestures and faces.[54] Some officials may have denied what they were trying to do, but the public knew full well the purpose of the new exhibit:

> There was always a crowd before the cage, most of the time roaring with laughter, and from almost every corner of the garden could be heard the question "Where is the

Pygmy?" and the answer was, "In the monkey house."[55]

The implications of the exhibit were also clear from the visitors' questions:

> Was he a man or monkey? Was he something in between? "Ist das ein Mensch?" asked a German spectator. "Is it a man?" . . . No one really mistook apes or parrots for human beings. This — it — came so much closer. Was it a man? Was it monkey? Was it a forgotten stage of evolution?[56]

One learned doctor even suggested that the exhibit should be used to help indoctrinate the public in the truth of evolution:

> It is a pity that Dr. Hornaday does not introduce the system of short lectures or talks in connection with such exhibitions. This would emphasize the scientific character of the service, enhance immeasurably the usefulness of the Zoological Park to our public in general, and help our clergymen to familiarize themselves with the scientific point of view so absolutely foreign to many of them.[57]

That he was on display was indisputable: a sign was posted on the enclosure which said:

> The African Pygmy, "Ota Benga." Age, 23 years. Height, 4 feet 11 inches. Weight 103

pounds. Brought from the Kasai River, Congo Free State, South Central Africa by Dr. Samuel P. Verner. Exhibited each afternoon during September.[58]

And what an exhibit it was.

> The orangutan imitated the man. The man imitated the monkey. They hugged, let go, flopped into each other's arms. Dohong [the orangutan] snatched the woven straw off Ota's head and placed it on his own. . . . the crowd hooted and applauded . . . children squealed with delight.
> To adults there was a more serious side to the display. Something about the boundary condition of being human was exemplified in that cage. Somewhere man shaded into non-human. Perhaps if they looked hard enough the moment of transition might be seen. . . . to a generation raised on talk of that absentee star of evolution, the Missing Link, the point of Dohong and Ota disporting in the monkey house was obvious.[59]

The point of the exhibit was also obvious to a *New York Times* reporter who stated:

> The Pygmy was not much taller than the orangutan, and one had a good opportunity to study their points of resemblance. Their heads are much alike, and both grin in the same way when pleased.[60]

That he was made much fun of is also indisputable: he was once given a pair of shoes, concerning which "over and over again the crowd laughed at him as he sat in mute admiration of them."[61] In another *New York Times* article one of the editors, after studying the situation, penned the following:

> Ota Benga . . . is a normal specimen of his race or tribe, with a brain as much developed as are those of its other members. Whether they are held to be illustrations of arrested development, and really closer to the anthropoid apes than the other African savages, or whether they are viewed as the degenerate descendants of ordinary negroes, they are of equal interest to the student of ethnology, and can be studied with profit. . . .
>
> As for Benga himself, he is probably enjoying himself as well as he could anywhere in this country, and it is absurd to make moan over the imagined humiliation and degradation he is suffering. The Pygmies are a fairly efficient people in their native forests . . . but they are very low in the human scale, and the suggestion that Benga should be in a school instead of a cage ignores the high probability that school would be a place of torture to him and one from which he could draw no advantage whatever. The idea that men are all much alike except as they have had or lacked opportunities for getting an education out of books is now far out of date. With training carefully adapted to his mental limitations,

this Pygmy could doubtless be taught many things . . . but there is no chance that he could learn anything in an ordinary school.[62]

That the display was extremely successful was never in doubt. Bradford and Blume claimed that on September 16, "40,000 visitors roamed the New York Zoological Park . . . the sudden surge of interest . . . was entirely attributable to Ota Benga." The crowds were so enormous that a police officer was assigned to guard Ota full-time (the zoo claimed this was to protect him) because he was "always in danger of being grabbed, yanked, poked, and pulled to pieces by the mob."[63]

Although it was widely believed at this time, even by eminent scientists, that blacks were evolutionarily inferior to Caucasians, caging one in a zoo produced much publicity and controversy, especially from ministers and Afro-Americans:

> The spectacle of a black man in a cage gave a *Times* reporter the springboard for a story that worked up a storm of protest among Negro ministers in the city. Their indignation was made known to Mayor George B. McClellan, but he refused to take action.[64]

When the storm of protests rose, Hornaday "saw no reason to apologize" stating that he "had the full support of the Zoological Society in what he was doing."[65] Evidently not many persons were very concerned about doing anything until the African-American community entered the foray. Although even some blacks at this time accepted the notion that the Pygmies were "defective specimens of mankind," several black ministers were determined to stop the exhibit.[66]

The use of the display to argue that blacks were an inferior race made them especially angry. Their concern was "they had heard blacks compared with apes often enough before; now the comparison was being played flagrantly at the largest zoo on earth." In Reverend Gordon's words, "Our race . . . is depressed enough without exhibiting one of us with the apes. We think we are worthy of being considered human beings, with souls."[67] Further, many of the ministers opposed the theory of evolution, concluding:

> The exhibition evidently aims to be a demonstration of the Darwinian theory of evolution. The Darwinian theory is absolutely opposed to Christianity, and a public demonstration in its favor should not be permitted.[68]

One *Times* article responded to the criticism that the display lent credibility to Darwinism with the following words:

> One reverend colored brother objects to the curious exhibition on the grounds that it is an impious effort to lend credibility to Darwin's dreadful theories . . . the reverend colored brother should be told that evolution . . . is now taught in the textbooks of all the schools, and that it is no more debatable than the multiplication table.[69]

Publishers Weekly commented that the creationist ministers were the only ones that "truly cared" about Ota.[70]

Soon some whites also became concerned about the "caged Negro," and in Sifakis' words, part of the concern was because "men of the cloth feared . . . that the Benga exhibition might be used to prove the Darwinian theory of evolution."[71] The objections were often vague, as in the words of a *New York Times* article:

> The exhibition was that of a human being in a monkey cage. The human being happened to be a Bushman, one of a race that scientists do not rate high in the human scale, but to the average non-scientific person in the crowd of sightseers there was something about the display that was unpleasant. It is probably a good thing that Benga doesn't think very deeply. If he did it isn't likely that he was very proud of himself when he woke in the morning and found himself under the same roof with the orangutans and monkeys, for that is where he really is.[72]

Some reporters, instead of ridiculing the zoo, criticized those who objected to the exhibit because they did not accept evolution. In Bradford and Blume's words, "New York scientists and preachers" wrangled over Ota, and those who believed that "humans were not descended from the apes and that Darwinism was an anti-Christian fraud . . . were subject to ridicule on the editorial pages of the *New York Times*."[73] Although opinions about the incident varied, they did result in many formal protests and threats of legal action to which the zoo director eventually acquiesced, and "finally . . . allowed the Pygmy out of his cage."[74] Once freed, Benga spent most of his time walking around the zoo grounds in a white suit, often with huge crowds following him. He returned to the monkey house only to sleep at night. Being treated as a curiosity, mocked, and made fun of by the visitors eventually caused Benga to "hate being mobbed by curious tourists and mean children."[75] In a letter to Verner, Hornaday revealed some of the many problems that the situation had caused:

> Of course we have not exhibited him [Benga] in the cage since the trouble began. Since dictating the above . . . Ota Benga . . . procured a carving knife from the feeding room of the monkey house, and went around the park flourishing it in a most alarming manner, and for a long time refused to give it up. Eventually it was taken away from him.
>
> Shortly after that he went to the soda fountain near the bird house, to get some soda, and because he was refused the soda he got into a great rage. . . . This led to a great fracas. He fought like a tiger, and it took three men to get him back to the monkey house. He has struck a number of visitors, and has "raised Cain" generally.[76]

He later "fashioned a little bow and a set of arrows and began shooting at zoo visitors he found particularly obnoxious!" *The New York Times* described the problem as follows:

There were 40,000 visitors to the park on Sunday. Nearly every man, woman and child of this crowd made for the monkey house to see the star attraction in the park – the wild man from Africa. They chased him about the grounds all day, howling, jeering, and yelling. Some of them poked him in the ribs, others tripped him up, all laughed at him.[77]

After Ota "wounded a few gawkers, he had to leave the Zoological Park for good."[78]

The resolution of the controversy, in Ward's words, came about because: "In the end Hornaday decided his prize exhibit had become more trouble than he was worth and turned him over to the Reverend Gordon, who also headed the Howard Colored Orphan Asylum in Brooklyn."[79]

Although Hornaday claimed that he was "merely offering an interesting exhibit and that Benga was happy. . . ." Milner notes that this "statement could not be confirmed"[80] since we have no record of Benga's feelings, but many of his actions reveal that he had adjusted poorly to zoo life. Unfortunately, Ota Benga did not leave any written records of his thoughts about this or anything else, thus the only side of the story that we have is Verner's voluminous records, the writings by Hornaday, the many newspaper accounts, and a 281-page book entitled *The Pygmy in the Zoo* by Philip Verner Bradford, Verner's grandson.

Bradford, in doing his research, had the good fortune that Verner saved virtually every letter that he had ever received, many of which discuss the Ota Benga situation, and all of which he had access to when doing his research. Interestingly, Verner related what he feels is the Pygmy view of evolution:

> After my acquaintance with the Pygmies had ripened into complete mutual confidence, I once made bold to tell them that some of the wise men of my country asserted that they had descended from the apes of the forest. This statement, far from provoking mirth, met with a storm of indignant protestation, and furnished the theme for many a heated discussion around the Batwa firesides. [81]

After Benga left the zoo, he was able to find care at a succession of institutions and with several sympathetic individuals, but he was never able to shed his freak-label history. First sent to a "colored" orphanage, Ota learned English and also took an interest in a certain young lady there, a woman named Creola. Unfortunately, even Ota's supporters believed some of the stories about him, and an "incident" soon took place which ignited a controversy. As a result, Ota was soon forever shuffled miles away from both Brooklyn and Creola.

In January 1910 he arrived at a black community in Lynchburg, Virginia, and there he seemed to shine.

> . . . black families [there] entrusted their young to Ota's care. They felt their boys were secure with him. He taught them to hunt, fish, gather wild honey. . . . The children felt safe when they were in the woods with him. If anything, they found him over-protective,

except in regard to gathering wild honey –
there was no such thing as too much pro-
tection when it came to raiding hives. . . . A
bee sting can feel catastrophic to a child,
but Ota couldn't help himself – he thought
bee stings were hilarious.[82]

He became a baptized Christian and his English
vocabulary rapidly improved. He also learned how
to read, and occasionally attended classes at a
Lynchburg seminary. He was popular among the
boys, and learned several sports such as baseball (at
which he did quite well). Every effort was made to
help him blend in (even his teeth were capped to help
him look more normal), and although he seemingly
had adjusted, inwardly he had not.

Several events and changes that occurred there
caused him to become despondent: after checking
on the price of steamship tickets to Africa, he concluded that he would never have enough money to
purchase one. He had not heard from Verner in a
while, and did not know how to contact him. He
later ceased attending classes and became a $10 a
month plus room and board laborer on the Obery
farm.[83] The school concluded that his lack of edu-
cational progress was because of his African "atti-
tude," but actually probably "his age was against his
development. It was simply impossible to put him
in a class to receive instructions . . . that would be of
any advantage to him."[84] He had enormous curiosity and a drive to learn, but preferred performance
tests as opposed to the multiple choice kind.

Later employed as a tobacco factory laborer in

Lynchburg, he grew increasingly depressed, hostile, irrational, and forlorn. When people spoke to him, they noticed that he had tears in his eyes when he told them he wanted to go home. Concluding that he would never be able to return to his native land, on March 20, 1916, Benga committed suicide with a revolver.[85] In Ward's words:

> Ota . . . removed the caps from his teeth. When his small companions asked him to lead them into the woods again, he turned them away. Once they were safely out of sight, he shot himself.[86]

To the end, Hornaday was inhumane, seriously distorting the situation, even slanderously stating that Ota "would rather die than work for a living."[87] In an account of his suicide published by Hornaday in the 1916 *Zoological Bulletin*, his evolution-inspired racist feelings clearly showed through:

> The young negro was brought to Lynchburg about six years ago, by some kindly disposed person, and was placed in the Virginia Theological Seminary and College here, where for several years *he labored to demonstrate to his benefactors that he did not possess the power of learning;* and some two or three years ago he quit the school and went to work as a laborer[88] (emphasis ours).

In Hornaday's words, Ota committed suicide because "the burden became so heavy that the young negro secured a revolver belonging to the woman with whom he lived, went to the cow stable and there sent a bullet through his heart, ending his life."[89]

How does Verner's grandson, a Darwinist himself, feel about the story? In his words, "The forest dwellers of Africa still arouse the interest of science. Biologists seek them out to test their blood and to bring samples of their DNA. They are drawn by new forms of the same questions that once vexed S.P. Verner and Chief McGee: What role do Pygmies play in human evolution? What relationship do they have to the original human type?" He adds that one clear difference does exist, and that is, "Today's evolutionists do not, like yesterday's anthropometricists, include demeaning comments and rough treatments in their studies." They now openly admit that the "triumph of Darwinism" was "soon after its inception [used] to reinforce every possible division by race, gender, and nationality." Part of the problem also was that "the press, like the public, was fascinated by, or addicted to, the spectacle of primitive man."[90] The tragedy, as Buhler expressed in a poem, is:

> From his native land of darkness, to the country of the free, in the interest of science .
> . . brought wee little Ota Benga . . . scarcely more than ape or monkey, yet a man the while.
> . . . Teach the freedom we have here in this land of foremost progress — in this Wisdom's ripest age — we have placed him, in high honor, in a monkey's cage! Mid companions we provide him, apes, gorillas, chimpanzees.[91]

(Note: The spelling in some of the quotes has been modernized.)

ENDNOTES

1 This chapter was researched and written by Dr. Jerry Bergman, Ph.D., Research Methodology from Wayne State University.

2 P.V. Bradford and H. Blume, *Ota Benga; The Pygmy in the Zoo* (New York: St. Martin's Press, 1992), p. 304.

3 T.G. Crookshank, *The Mongol in Our Midst* (New York: E. F. Dutton, 1924).

4 J. Bergman, "Eugenics and the Development of the Nazi Race Policy," *Perspectives on Science and Christian Faith*, vol. 44, no. 2, June 1992, p. 109–123.

   J. Bergman, "Censorship in Secular Science; The Mims Case," *Perspectives on Science and Christian Faith*, March 1993, vol. 45, no. 1, p. 37–45.

5 Bradford and Blume, *Ota Benga; The Pygmy in the Zoo*, p. 40.

6 Ibid., p. 41.

7 James H. Birx, "Ota Benga: The Pygmy in the Zoo," *Library Journal*, vol. 117, no. 13, August 1992, p. 134.

8 C. Sifakis, "Benga, Ota: The Zoo Man," *American Eccentrics* (New York: Facts on File, 1984), p. 252–253.

9 W. Bridges, *Gathering of Animals; An Unconventional History of the New York Zoological Society* (New York: Harper and Row Publishers, 1974).

10 Bradford and Blume, *Ota Benga; The Pygmy in the Zoo*, p. 94–95.

11 Ibid., p. 113.

12 S.P. Verner, "The African Pygmies," *Popular Science*, vol. 69, 1906, p. 471–473.

13 Munn and Company, editors, "The Government Philippine Expedition," *Scientific American*, July 23, 1904, p. 107–108.

14 Bradford and Blume, *Ota Benga; The Pygmy in the Zoo*, p. 113–114.

15 Ibid., p. 121.

16 A. Gatti, *Great Mother Forest* (New York: Charles Scribner's Sons, 1937).

17 Bradford and Blume, *Ota Benga; The Pygmy in the Zoo*, p. 122.
18 Ibid., p. 16.
19 Munn, 1904, p. 64.
20 Munn and Company, editors, "Pygmies of the Congo." *Scientific American*, vol. 93, August 5, 1905, p. 107–108.
21 Bradford and Blume, *Ota Benga; The Pygmy in the Zoo*, p. 118–119.
22 Ibid., p. 104.
23 Ibid., p. 106.
24 Ibid., p. 110.
25 S.P. Verner, "The White Man's Zone in Africa," *World's Work*, vol. 13, 1906, p. 8227–8236.
26 Bradford and Blume, *Ota Benga; The Pygmy in the Zoo*, p. 176.
27 "Negro Ministers Act to Free Pygmy; Will Ask the Mayor to Have Him Taken From Monkey Cage. Committee Visits the Zoo; Public Exhibitions of the Dwarf Discontinued, But Will Be Resumed, Mr. Hornaday Says," *New York Times*, September 11, 1906, p. 2.
28 Bradford and Blume, *Ota Benga; The Pygmy in the Zoo*, p. 174.
29 Ibid., p. 180.
30 Sifakis, "Benga, Ota: The Zoo Man," p. 253.
31 Bradford and Blume, *Ota Benga; The Pygmy in the Zoo*, p. 181.
32 W.T. Hornaday, "An African Pygmy," *Zoological Society Bulletin*, vol. 23, October 1906, p. 302.
33 Ibid. p. 301–302.
34 R. Rymer, "Darwinism, Barnumism, and Racism," "Ota Benga: The Pygmy in the Zoo," *The New York Times Book Review*, September 6, 1992, p. 3.
35 S.P. Verner, "The White Race in the Tropics," *World's Work*, vol. 16, 1908, p. 10717.
36 Jean-Pierre Hallet, *Pygmy Kitabu* (New York: Random House, 1973), p. 292, 358–359.
37 Bradford and Blume, *Ota Benga; The Pygmy in the Zoo*, p. 20.
38 Ibid.

39 A.H.J. Keane, "Anthropological Curiosities; the Pygmies of the World," *Scientific American*, vol. 64, supplement no. 1650, July 6, 1907, p. 99.

40 Guy Burrows, *The Land of the Pygmies* (New York: Thomas Y. Crowell & Co., 1905), p. 172, 182.

41 H.H. Johnston, "Pygmies of the Great Congo Forest," *Smithsonian Report*, 1902, p. 479–491.
    H.H. Johnston, "Pygmies of the Great Congo Forest," *Current Literature*, vol. 32, 1902, p. 294-295.
    A.B. Lloyd, "Through Dwarf Land and Cannibal Country," *Athenaeum*, vol. 2, 1899, p. 894–895.

42 C. Turnbull, *The Forest People* (New York: Simon and Schuster, 1968).

43 Caroline Furness Jayne, *String Figures and How To Make Them* (New York: Dover Publishers, 1962), p. 276, reprinted from the original publication: Caroline (Furness) Jayne, *String Figures* (New York: Charles Scribner's Sons, 1906).

44 Hallet, *Pygmy Kitabu*, p. 14–15.

45 Bradford and Blume, *Ota Benga; The Pygmy in the Zoo*, p. 69–70.

46 S.P. Verner, "The African Pygmies," *Atlantic*, vol. 90, 1902, p. 192.

47 Ibid., p. 193.

48 Bradford and Blume, *Ota Benga; The Pygmy in the Zoo*, p. 69, p.70, 72, 74.

49 Verner, "The White Race in the Tropics," p. 10718.

50 Verner, "The African Pygmies," p. 189–190.

51 Verner, "The White Man's Zone in Africa," p. 8235.
    S.P. Verner, "Africa Fifty Years Hence," *World's Work*, vol. 13, 1907, p. 8736.

52 S.P. Verner, "An Education Experiment with Cannibals," *World's Work*, vol. 4, 1902, p. 2289–2295.

53 Bradford and Blume, *Ota Benga; The Pygmy in the Zoo*, p. 175.

54 Ibid., p. 180.

55 "Man and Monkey Show Disapproved by Clergy; The Rev. Dr. MacArthur Thinks the Exhibition Degrading; Colored Ministers to Act; The Pygmy Has an Orangutan as

a Companion Now and Their Antics Delight the Bronx Crowds," *New York Times*, September 10, 1906, p.1.

56 Bradford and Blume, *Ota Benga; The Pygmy in the Zoo*, p. 179.

57 M.S. Gabriel, "Ota Benga Having a Fine Time; A Visitor at the Zoo Finds No Reason For Protests About the Pygmy," *New York Times*, September 13, 1906, p. 6.

58 "Man and Monkey Show Disapproved by Clergy. . . ."

59 Bradford and Blume, *Ota Benga; The Pygmy in the Zoo*, p. 181.

60 "Man and Monkey Show Disapproved by Clergy. . . ."

61 Ibid.

62 "Topic of the Times; Send Him Back to the Woods," *New York Times*, September 11, 1906, p. 6.

63 Bradford and Blume, *Ota Benga; The Pygmy in the Zoo*, p. 185, 187.

64 Bridges, *Gathering of Animals: An Unconventional History of the New York Zoological Society*, p. 224.

65 Bradford and Blume, *Ota Benga; The Pygmy in the Zoo*, p. 182.

66 "Man and Monkey Show Disapproved by Clergy. . . ."

67 "Negro Ministers Act to Free Pygmy. . . ."

68 Bradford and Blume, *Ota Benga; The Pygmy in the Zoo*, p. 183.

69 "Topics of the Times; The Pigmy Is Not the Point," *New York Times*, September 12, 1906, p. 8.

70 "Ota Benga: The Pygmy in the Zoo," Review in *Publishers Weekly*, vol. 239, no. 23, July 27, 1992, p. 56.

71 Sifakis, "Benga, Ota: The Zoo Man," p. 253.

72 "Bushman Shares a Cage With Bronx Park Apes; Some Laugh Over His Antics, But Many Are Not Pleased; Keeper Frees Him at Times; Then, With Bow and Arrow, the Pygmy From the Congo Takes to the Woods," *New York Times*, September 9, 1906, p. 9.

73 Bradford and Blume, *Ota Benga; The Pygmy in the Zoo*, p. 191, 196.

74 Sifakis, "Benga, Ota: The Zoo Man," p. 253.

75 R. Milner, *The Encyclopedia of Evolution: Humanity's Search For Its Origins*, (New York: Facts on File, Inc., 1990), p. 42.

76 Bridges, *Gathering of Animals: An Unconventional History of the New York Zoological Society*, p. 227–228.

77 "African Pygmy's Fate Is Still Undecided; Director Hornaday of the Bronx Park Throws Up His Hands; Asylum Doesn't Take Him; Benga Meanwhile Laughs and Plays with a Ball and Mouth Organ at the Same Time," *New York Times*, September 18, 1906, p. 9.

78 Milner, *The Encyclopedia of Evolution: Humanity's Search For Its Origins.*

79 G.C. Ward, "Ota Benga: The Pygmy in the Zoo" *American Heritage*, vol. 43, October 1992, p. 12–14.

80 Milner, *The Encyclopedia of Evolution: Humanity's Search For Its Origins.*

81 Verner, "The African Pygmies," p. 190.

82 Bradford and Blume, *Ota Benga; The Pygmy in the Zoo*, p. 206–207.

83 Ibid., p. 204.

84 Ward, "Ota Benga: The Pygmy in the Zoo."

85 E.R. Sanborn, editor, "Suicide of Ota Benga, the African Pygmy," *Zoological Society Bulletin*, vol. 19, no. 3, May 1916, p. 1356.

86 Ward, "Ota Benga: The Pygmy in the Zoo."

87 Bradford and Blume, *Ota Benga; The Pygmy in the Zoo*, p. 220.

88 W.T. Hornaday, "Suicide of Ota Benga, The African Pygmy," *Zoological Society Bulletin*, vol. 19, no. 3, May 1916, p. 1356.

89 Ibid.

90 Bradford and Blume, *Ota Benga; The Pygmy in the Zoo*, p. xx, 7, 230–231.

91 M.E. Buhler, "Ota Benga," *New York Times*, September 19, 1906, p. 8.

CHAPTER 11

HOW TO BECOME A MEMBER OF THE LAST ADAM'S "RACE"

As we have clearly shown, we are all of one race. Because the Bible's account of the history of the human race is true, each person needs to be confronted with the consequences of our history.

The Bible tells us that we have inherited a sinful (rebellious) nature from the first man Adam which separates us from our Creator. We are all in need of salvation, which comes from the last Adam, Jesus Christ (our Creator who stepped into history to be our Savior). We can receive the free gift of salvation resulting in eternal life with our Creator.

The Bible says there are five things we need to

know about receiving eternal life.

1. *Eternal life (heaven) is a gift.* The Bible says: "The gift of God is eternal life through Jesus Christ our Lord" (Rom. 6:23). Like any other genuine gift, it is not earned or deserved. No amount of personal effort, good works, or religious deeds can earn a place in heaven.

The Bible also states in Ephesians 2:8–9 that "For by grace you are saved through faith, and that not of yourselves, it is the gift of God, not of works, lest anyone should boast."

Why is it that no one can earn his or her way to heaven? It is because . . .

2. *All humans are sinners:* "For all have sinned and come short of the glory of God" (Rom. 3:23).

Sin is transgressing God's law and includes such things as lying, lusting, cheating, deceit, anger, evil thoughts, immoral behavior, and more. Because we are sinners, we cannot save ourselves. In fact, do you know how good you would have to be to save yourself by your own good deeds? Matthew 5:48 declares: "Therefore be perfect, even as your Father in heaven is perfect."

Perfection is such a high standard that no one can save himself. However, in spite of our sin . . .

3. *God is merciful:* 1 John 4:8 says that "God is love" and in Jeremiah 31:3 He says, "I have loved you with an everlasting love."

Because God loves us, He doesn't want to punish us. God, however, is also just and therefore must punish sin. He says: "Who will by no means clear the guilty" (Exod. 34:7) and "The soul that sins, it shall die" (Ezek. 18:4).

We have a problem! Despite God's love for us, His justice demands that He must punish our sin. But there is a remedy . . .

4. *Jesus Christ is the solution.* The Bible tells us that Christ is the infinite God-Man. "In the beginning was the Word [Jesus], and the Word [Jesus] was God. . . . And the Word [Jesus] became flesh, and tabernacled among us" (John 1:1–14).

Jesus Christ — the last Adam — came to earth and lived a sinless life. He died on the cross to pay the penalty for our sins and rose from the grave to purchase a place for us in heaven. "All we like sheep have gone astray; we have turned, each one to his own way; and the Lord has laid on Him the iniquity of us all" (Isa. 53:6).

Jesus Christ bore our sin in His body on the cross and now offers you eternal life (heaven) as a gift (1 Pet. 2:24). How?

5. *This gift is received by faith.* Faith is the key that opens the door to heaven. Many people, however, mistake two things for saving faith:

> a. Believing that an intelligent designer or creator exists. However, the Bible says that even the devil believes in God (James 2:19); therefore, just believing in God is not saving faith.

> b. Having temporal faith, such as trusting God to solve temporary crises, including financial, family, or physical needs. While it is good to trust Christ to meet these needs, this is not saving faith.

Saving faith is trusting in Jesus Christ *alone* for eternal life. It means resting upon Christ alone and what *He* has done on the cross, rather than what you or I have done. "And they said, Believe on the Lord Jesus Christ and you shall be saved, and your household" (Acts 16:31).

The question that God would ask of non-believers is: Would you like to receive the gift of eternal life? You would need to transfer your trust from what you have been doing to what Christ has done for you on His cross, and then confess, "Because if you confess the Lord Jesus, and believe in your heart that God has raised Him from the dead, you shall be saved" (Rom. 10:9).

Acts 3:19 says that you should "Therefore repent and convert so that your sins may be blotted out." Repentence is not only a heartfelt, sorrowful remorse for past sins, but also a change of mind, which is proven by a changed life.

If you wish to repent, have your sins blotted out, and receive Christ as Savior, here is a suggested prayer:

> Jesus Christ, I know I am a sinner and do not deserve eternal life. But I believe You died to pay for my sins and rose from the grave to purchase a place in heaven for me.
>
> Lord Jesus, come into my life — take control of my life — forgive my sins and save me. I repent of my sins and now place my trust in You alone for my salvation. I desire to receive the free gift of eternal life.

If you have prayed this prayer of repentance, and sincerely meant it, you have received the gift of eternal life! You are now a child of God — and no one can take that from you — forever.

Just as a newborn baby grows physically, so now you need to grow spiritually. Read your Bible, starting perhaps with the Gospel of John, reading at least one chapter a day. Then read the first 11 chapters of the foundational Book of Genesis. Also, spend some time talking (praying) with God.

It is also important that you regularly attend a Bible-believing church that honors Christ and teaches that the Bible is the inspired Word of God and is authoritative for every aspect of your life (2 Tim. 3:15). Seek the fellowship of Christians that can help you grow in your faith. And as you grow, tell others what Christ means to you.

If you have found new life through Christ through this book, please email us at

mail@answersingenesis.org

or write to one of the Answers in Genesis ministries at the back of the book.

WHY DOES
IT MATTER?

Many years ago in Australia, a Bible col
lege student declared that missionaries
should not waste their time preaching to
the Australian Aborigines. He believed they weren't
of Adam's race, and therefore could not be saved.[1]

Sadly, history reports that some missionaries
didn't see the need to take the gospel message to certain "primitive" tribes because they were not suffi-
ciently "human" on the evolutionary scale. For instance, a professor in the 1800's wrote:

> If one must draw a sharp boundary be-
> tween them, it has to be drawn between the
> most highly developed and civilized man on
> the one hand and the rudest savages on the
> other, and the latter have to be classed with
> the animals. This is, in fact, the opinion of
> many travelers, who have long watched the
> lowest human races in their native countries.
> Thus, for example, a great English traveler,
> who lived for a considerable time on the west
> coast of Africa, says: "I consider the Negro

to be a lower species of man, and cannot make up my mind to look upon him as 'a man and a brother,' for the gorilla would then also have to be admitted into the family." Even many Christian missionaries, who, after long years of fruitless endeavors to civilize these lowest races have abandoned the attempt, express the same harsh judgment and maintain that it would be easier to train the most intelligent domestic animals to a moral and civilized life, than these unreasoning brute-like men. For instance, the able Austrian missionary Morlang, who tried for many years without the slightest success to civilize the ape-like Negro tribes on the Upper Nile, expressly says: "that any mission to such savages is absolutely useless. They stand far below unreasoning animals; the latter at least show signs of affection towards those who are kind towards them, whereas these brutal natives are utterly incapable of any feeling of gratitude.[2]

Evolutionists like Hitler treated the Jews, Gypsies, and other groups as inferior, and therefore argued that they needed to be eliminated.[3]

Today, depending on the country, marriages between different people groups often result in persecution for the parents and the children. In addition, current attempts at "ethnic cleansing" are the result of the hatred of one particular people group toward another. Even within a segment of the Church in America today, there remains intense prejudice in regard to one's skin shade.

All of these problems, and any others concerning such "racial" prejudice, could easily be solved if all people built their thinking on God's Word, and would believe:

> And He has made all nations of men of *one blood* to dwell on all the face of the earth, ordaining fore-appointed seasons and boundaries of their dwelling (Acts 17:26).

The point is that *all* human beings are descendants of Adam; *all* need to build their thinking on God's Word and accept that they are sinners in need of salvation; *all* need to judge their behavior in every area, regardless of their culture, against the absolute standards of the Word of God; and *all* need to repent and receive the free gift of salvation.

We *all* need to treat every human being as our relative (we're of "one blood"), and recognize that all of us are equal in value before our Creator God. What a difference it would make in this world if each person understood and adopted this biblical principle! Then each of us could proclaim with the apostle Paul:

> For there is no difference both of Jew and of Greek, for the same Lord over all is rich to all who call on Him (Rom. 10:12).

ENDNOTES

[1] Personal conversation between Ken Ham and a Bible college student in Brisbane, Australia, 1983.

[2] Ernst Haeckel, *The History of Creation: Vol. II*, Translated by E. Ray Lancaster, Henry S. King & Co., London, 1876, p. 365-6.

[3] Jerry Bergman, "Darwinism and the Nazi race Holocaust," *Technical Journal*, Vol. 13, No. 2, 1999, p. 101-111.

FOR ADDITIONAL REFERENCES ON OTA BENGA SEE:

Jerry Bergman, "Ota Benga: The Story of the Pygmy on Display in the Zoo," *Creation Research Society Quarterly*, vol. 30, no. 3, December 1993, p. 140–149.

Jerry Bergman, "Ota Benga; The Story of an African Pygmy on Display in a Zoo," *Destiny*, December 1994, p. 24–25.

Samuel P. Verner, "Development of Africa," *Forum*, vol. 32, 1901, p. 366–382.

Samuel P. Verner, "Affairs of the Congo State," *Forum*, vol. 36, 1904, p. 150–159.

Samuel P. Verner, "Bringing the Pygmies to America," *Independent*, vol. 57, 1904, p. 485–489.

Samuel P. Verner, "How the Batwa Pygmies Were Brought to the St. Louis Fair," *Harpers Weekly*, 48, 1904, p.1618–1620.

Samuel P. Verner, "Pioneering in Central Africa," Review, *Nation*, 78, 1904, p. 357–358; H.A. Coblentz, *Dial*, vol. 36, p. 363–364; *Independent*, vol. 57, p. 739.

Samuel P. Verner, "The Adventures of an Explorer in Africa; How the Pygmies Were Brought to the St. Louis Fair," *Harper's Weekly*, October 22, 1904, p.1618–1620.

Samuel P. Verner, "African Pygmies," *Scientific American*, supplement, vol. 59, no. 24, 1905, p. 567–568.

Samuel P. Verner, "American Invasion of the Congo," *Harper's Weekly,* vol. 51, 1907, p. 644.

Samuel P. Verner, "Belgian Rule on the Congo," *World's Work*, vol. 13, 1907, p. 8568–8575.

Samuel P. Verner, "The Story of Ota Benga, the Pygmy," *Zoological Society Bulletin*, vol. 19, no. 4, July 1916, p.1377–1379.

NEWSPAPER ARTICLES ON OTA BENGA IN ST. LOUIS

"African Pygmies for the World's Fair; Amazing Dwarfs of the Congo Valley to be Seen in St Louis. Some Red, Some black. They Antedate the Negro in Equatorial Africa. Fearless

Midgets Who Boldly Attack Elephants with Tiny Lances, Bows and Arrows," *St. Louis Post-Dispatch*, June 26, 1904.

"An Untold Chapter of My Adventures While Hunting Pygmies in Africa, by Samuel P. Verner," *St. Louis Post-Dispatch*, September 4, 1904.

"Barbarians Meet in Athletic Games; Pygmies in Mud Fight, Pelted Each Other Until One Side Was Put to Rout. Crow Indian Won Mile Run; Negritos Captured Pole-Climbing Event and Patagonians Beat Syrians in Tug-of-War," *St. Louis Post-Dispatch*, August 6, 1904.

"Cannibals Will Sing and Dance," *St. Louis Post-Dispatch*, August 6, 1904.

"Driven From Huts by Rainstorm; Pygmies and Ainus Seek Shelter for Night in Indian School; Resembles Noah's Ark; Savages Insist on Taking Pets from Jungle Homes with Them to Escape Terrors of Lightning," *St. Louis Republic*, August 20, 1904.

"Enraged Pygmies Attack Visitor; H. S. Gibbons of Durango Colorado Photographed Them, But Gave No Tips. He Was Pursued and Beaten; Money Would Have Been an Effective Weapon, But He Wouldn't Use It," *St. Louis Post-Dispatch*, July 19, 1904.

"Exposition Envoy Pygmies' Victim? Fair Officials Have Not heard for Two Months from Explorer Sent to African Wilds. Tribe Uses Deadly Arrows; Perilous Undertaking of Anthropological Department Approved by Belgian Colonial Government," *St. Louis Post-Dispatch*, April 18, 1904.

"Gifts to Royal Pair Cost $2.50; President Francis Makes Happy the Hearts of World's Fair Pygmies for $8.35. Barrel of Salt for King; and other Presents of Similar Value are Given Little Africans Before Departure," *St. Louis Post-Dispatch*, December 4, 1904.

"Pygmies Demand a Monkey Diet; Gentlemen from South Africa at the Fair Likely to Prove Troublesome in Matter of Food," *St. Louis Dispatch*, July 2, 1904.

"Pygmies Shiver Over Camp Fire; 'Give Us Blankets,' is Their Greeting to Missionary Who Brought Them Out of Africa. Say It's Cold in St. Louis; Discard Palm Leaf Suits for Warmer Clothing — Declare Americans Treat Them as They Would Monkeys," *St. Louis Republic*, August 6, 1904.

"Pygmy Dance Starts Panic in Fair Plaza; Seeing Unclad Africans Advancing Toward Her, Brandishing Their Spears, Woman Screams and Crowd Follows Her in Terror," *St. Louis Post-Dispatch*, July 1904.

"10,000 Strange People for Fair; The World's Fair Pike Will Soon Be the Most Cosmopolitan Spot on Face of the Earth. Whole Shiploads en Route; Furthermost Corners of the Earth Are to Be Represented by Natives in Their Characteristic Splendor," *St. Louis Post-Dispatch*, April 1, 1904.

"To Exhibit Man at the St. Louis Fair; Dr. McGee Gathering Types and Freaks from Every Land. He Explains the Plans of the Department of Anthropology, of Which He Is the Head," *New York Times*, November 16, 1904.

"Trying Ordeal for Savages; Scientists Will Begin a Special Study of World's Fair Tribes September 1," *St. Louis Republic*, August 14, 1904.

"Verner Escapes Being Eaten by Cannibals; Man Who Went in Quest of African Pygmies Cables Exposition Company," *St. Louis Republic*, May 5, 1904.

"World's Fair Department of Anthropology: Portions of Ancient Cities Are to Be Represented and Unwritten History Revealed. Treasures of Antiquity Will Be So Arranged as to Show the Bearing Man's Past Achievements Have Upon Contemporary Progress," *St. Louis Republic*, March 6, 1904.

NEWSPAPER ARTICLES ON OTA BENGA IN NEW YORK

"A Pygmy Among the Primates; One of the 'Bantams' of the African Race at the Zoological Park — His Diversions — Twenty-Three, and Twice married — To Return to Africa Later," [New York] *Evening Post*, September 10, 1906.

"A Word For Benga; Mr. Verner Asks New York Not to Spoil His Friend, the Bushman," *New York Daily Tribune*, October 3, 1906.

"Benga." *New York Times*, September 23, 1906, editorial, p. 8.

"Benga Tries to Kill; Pygmy Slashes at Keeper Who Objected to His Garb," *New York Daily Tribune*, September 26, 1906.

"Colored Orphan Home Gets the Pygmy; He Has a Room to Himself and May Smoke if He Likes. To Be Educated If Possible; When He Returns to the Congo He May Then Help to Civilize His People," *New York Times*, September 29, 1906, p. 7.

"Escaped the Gridiron; Pygmy Man Saved from Cannibals Visits New York," *New York Daily Tribune*, September 16, 1906.

"Hope for Ota Benga; If Little, He's No Fool; And Has Good Reason For Staying in the White Man's Land. Won't Be An Entree Here; But His Chief In Africa May Die Soon and the Custom Is to Have a Cannibal Feast," *New York Times*, September 30, 1906, p. 9.

"Lively Row Over Pygmy," *New York Times*, September 10, 1906.

"M'Clellan Snubs Colored Ministers; Curtly Refuses to Receive Protest Against Exhibition of Man in Ape Cage," *New York American*, September 12, 1906.

"Negro Clergy Protest; Displeased at Exhibition of Bushman in Monkey House," *New York Daily Tribune*, September 11, 1906, p. 6.

"No Aid From M'Clellen; Mayor 'Too Busy' to See Committee of Colored Men; They Visited to Protest Against the Public Exhibition of a Negro Dwarf in the Monkey House at the Zoological Park — The Delegation Told by a Subordinate to Complain to the New York Zoological Society," *The* [New York] *Evening Post*, September 11, 1906.

"Ota Benga at Hippodrome; Pygmy Meets His Old Friend, the Baby Elephant, Giving Out Programmes," *New York Daily Tribune*, October 3, 1906.

"Ota Benga Now a Real Colored Gentleman; Little African Pygmy Being Taught Ways of Civilization at Howard Colored Orphan Asylum," *New York Daily Globe*, October 16, 1906.

"Ota Benga, Pygmy Tired of America; The Strange Little African Finally Ended Life at Lynchburg, VA. Once at the Bronx Zoo; His American Sponsor Found Him Shrewd and Courageous — Wanted to be Educated," *New York Times*, July 16, 1916, p. 12.

"Ota Benga Says Civilization Is All Witchcraft; On Exhibition at the New York Zoological Park, in Bronx, He Rules

Monkey House by Jungle Dread. Wants to Go Home to Buy Him a Wife; African Pygmy Asserts New York Is Not Wonderful and that We Are All Madmen," *New York World*, September 16, 1906.

"Pygmy to Be Kept Here; Colored Ministers Want to Take Him When Guardian Comes," *New York Times*, September 19, 1906, p. 1.

"Still Stirred About Benga," *New York Times*, September 23, 1906, p. 9.

"The Black Pigmy in the Monkey Cage; An Exhibition in Bad Taste, Offensive to Honest Men, and Unworthy of New York City's Government," *New York Journal*, September 17, 1906.

"The Mayor Won't Help to Free Caged Pygmy; He Refers Negro Ministers to the Zoological Society. Crowd Annoys the Dwarf; Failing to Get Action from Other Sources the Committee Will Ask the Courts to Interfere," *New York Times*, September 12, 1906, p. 9.

"Topics of the Times; Send Him Back to the Woods," *New York Times*, September 11, 1906, p. 6.

"Zoo Has A Pygmy Too Many; Does Anybody Want this Orphan Boarder? He Does Not Bite, He Does Not Vote, His Manners, Though Various, are Mild — Prof. Verner, African Traveler, Why Don't You Come and Get Him?" *New York Sun*, September 17, 1906.

FAITH-BUILDING RESOURCES ON A VARIETY OF TOPICS

"Ape-men"

Bones of Contention — Dr. Marvin Lubenow (Grand Rapids, MI: Baker Book House, 1992). One of the best and most recent publications to refute the so-called "ape-men."

Commentary

The Genesis Record — Dr. Henry Morris (Grand Rapids, MI: Baker Book House, 1979). The classic work by the founder of the modern creationist movement.

Creation vs. evolution

The Answers Book, updated and expanded — Ken Ham, Dr. Carl Wieland, and Dr. Jonathan Sarfati, edited by Dr. Don Batten (Green Forest, AR: Master Books, 2000). The 20 most-asked questions on Genesis answered (dinosaurs, continental drift, starlight and time, etc.).

"Answers with Ken Ham" video series — 12 videos, each well illustrated, answering 12 frequently asked questions (How do we know God exists? Are dinosaurs in the Bible? etc.) (Answers in Genesis).

Refuting Evolution — Dr. Jonathan Sarfati (Green Forest, AR: Master Books, 1999). Easy-to-understand, up-to-date arguments against evolution and for creation!

The Young Earth — Dr. John Morris (Green Forest, AR: Master Books, 1994). Dr. Morris, a geologist, explains in easy-to-understand terms how science supports a young Earth.

Dinosaurs

The Great Dinosaur Mystery Solved! — Ken Ham (Green Forest, AR: Master Books, 1998). How dinosaurs fit with the Bible, not evolution! An excellent way to teach the real history of the world using dinosaurs!

Races/racism

"One Blood: The Biblical Answer to Racism" video – Ken Ham. A docu-lecture of this book (Answers in Genesis).

Relevance of creation

The Lie: Evolution — Ken Ham (Green Forest, AR: Master Books, 1987). The best-selling book on the importance of the creation/evolution debate to the church and society!

Creation magazine — a quarterly faith-building magazine, with dozens of colorful photographs (Answers in Genesis).

"The Genesis Solution" video — Ken Ham. This acclaimed film — highly animated — shows why Christians must believe the Bible from the very first verse (Answers in Genesis).

Witnessing

Creation Evangelism for the New Millennium — Ken Ham (Green Forest, AR: Master Books, 1999). How to effectively witness to an anti-Christian, humanistic society!

Dinosaurs and the Bible (booklet) — Ken Ham. The most-asked questions about dinosaurs are answered. Also suitable as a witnessing booklet (Answers in Genesis).

Is There Really a God? — Ken Ham. A great witnessing booklet to share with your family and friends that God exists and that "His fingerprints" are all over our world (Answers in Genesis).

FOR FURTHER INFORMATION

For a free catalog of material supporting biblical creation, or for more information about what the Bible teaches, contact one of the Answers in Genesis ministries below. Answers in Genesis ministries are evangelical, Christ-centered, non-denominational, and non-profit.

Answers in Genesis
P.O. Box 6330
Florence, KY 41022
USA

Answers in Genesis
P.O. Box 6302
Acacia Ridge DC
QLD 4110
Australia

Answers in Genesis
5-420 Erb St. West
Suite 213
Waterloo, Ontario
Canada N2L 6K6

Answers in Genesis
P.O. Box 39005
Howick, Auckland
New Zealand

Answers in Genesis
P.O. Box 5262
Leicester LE2 3XU
United Kingdom

Answers in Genesis
Attn: Nao Hanada
3317-23 Nagaoka, Ibaraki-machi
Higashi-ibaraki-gun, Ibaraki-ken 311-3116
Japan

In addition, you may contact:

Institute for Creation Research
P.O. Box 2667
El Cajon, CA 92021

For further information on creation evangelism, creation/evolution, dinosaurs, a wide variety of "hot topics," free transparency masters, recent AiG newsletters, *Creation* magazine, and the *Creation ex nihilo Technical Journal* and more, check out our popular and attractive Website at:

www.AnswersInGenesis.org

ABOUT THE AUTHORS

Ken Ham is the founder and executive director of Answers in Genesis - U.S. He is one of the most in-demand Christian speakers in North America. Ken is the author of many books and is the host of a daily radio program called *Answers . . . with Ken Ham* (heard on more than 300 stations worldwide).

Dr. Carl Wieland is the managing director of Answers in Genesis - Australia. He is the founder and editor of AiG's full-color *Creation* magazine (for which he also contributes numerous articles), and is the author of the popular layperson booklet *Stones and Bones*.

Dr. Don Batten is a consultant plant physiologist and research scientist who now works full-time for Answers in Genesis in Brisbane, Australia, as a speaker, writer, and researcher.

CREATION EVANGELISM FOR THE NEW MILLENNIUM

by Ken Ham

The first of its kind, this book offers a bold approach to evangelism by looking at the effects of evolutionary compromise on the modern Church, and how to reverse the dangerous trend. Ham alerts church leaders and laypersons that a low view of Genesis among Christian leaders is rendering the Church ineffective at evangelism in our modern world.

A non-denominational work, this book clearly explains the foundational importance of Genesis.

ISBN: 0-89051-247-7
176 pages
$10.99

Available at Christian bookstores nationwide

THE LIE:
EVOLUTION

by Ken Ham

The Bible prophetically warns that in the last days false teachers will introduce destructive lies among the people. Their purpose is to bring God's truth into disrepute and to exploit believers by telling them made-up and imagined stories (see 2 Pet. 2:1–3).

An eye-opening look at the harmful effects of evolutionary thought on modern culture and religion. Author Ken Ham uses his years of teaching and ministry experience to expose false teaching that is destroying children and families.

ISBN: 0-89051-158-6
192 pages
$9.95

Available at Christian bookstores nationwide

GENESIS AND THE DECAY OF THE NATIONS

by Ken Ham

The perfect introduction for readers interested in the question of origins, this book emphasizes that the foundations of home and country are found in the Book of Beginnings. Especially helpful for church leaders, this book can lay a foundation for further study.

ISBN: 0-89051-275-2
96 pages
$6.95

Available at Christian bookstores nationwide